# PRAISE FOR
## *RAISING KIDS BEYOND THE BINARY*

"Jamie and Rebekah Bruesehoff are real-life heroes. Not only do they demonstrate immense bravery in all of their actions; they are changing the world one giant step at a time. They teach us that, whatever your religion, love is universal, and everyone deserves the freedom to express who they are authentically. Rebekah has grown to become a wise, mature, and beautiful young woman, and I'm so incredibly proud of her. Thank you for always being you."

—**Jazz Jennings**, LGBTQ rights activist, author of
*Being Jazz*, and star of the TLC series *I Am Jazz*

"For any person who loves someone who is transgender or gender diverse, this is a book for you! Each page is an opportunity to find reflections of your own story, be encouraged through powerful and vulnerable sharing, learn something new, and, most importantly, know you are not alone. Don't miss the chance to deepen and expand the wholeness of your family and loved ones. This is a profound and timely read."

—**Aubrey Thonvold**, executive director, ReconcilingWorks

"As a gay dad, my number-one priority is raising kids who love themselves wholly and show kindness and empathy for others. Which is why I'm so grateful for Jamie Bruesehoff's honest, wise, and personal new book, *Raising Kids Beyond the Binary*. This book is for every parent who wants to help their kids navigate healthy conversations and curiosities about gender. Bruesehoff's personal insight has not only given me language and guidance for engaging the topic of gender but has equipped and empowered me to know better how to help my kids love and support their transgender and nonbinary friends well."

—**Matthew Paul Turner**, author of the #1 *New York Times*–bestselling books *What Is God Like?* and *When God Made You*

"When I think someone wants or needs to be enlightened about the trans reality, I will recommend this book. Part memoir, part storytelling, and part instruction, this book both enlightens and inspires. I also believe it will change hearts and minds and help us all envision and create a more intelligent, inclusive, and compassionate world. Plus, we meet Jamie's trans daughter, the Mighty Rebekah, and read her own words about her experience and her vision for humanity. I'm so happy this book exists. What a resource!"

—**David Hayward**, artist @NakedPastor and author of *Flip It Like This!*

"Reading Jamie Brueshoff's *Raising Kids Beyond the Binary* is like sitting down with Jamie in her living room, having her take your hand, inviting you to learn with her, lean on her, and feeling like you have known her for years and trust her like a dear friend. For any parent or caregiver eager to better understand their child's gender journey, Jamie is a skilled, engaging teacher who makes an often-complex topic accessible and clear; there are dozens of aha moments along the path. Jamie's clarion call is to live with love and grace, and literally every page is rooted in this value. Having read many books and articles on this topic and talked with hundreds of parents of trans and nonbinary youth, I can confidently say this book is *essential* reading. It is the premier primer for any parent or other adult looking for guidance on raising their gender-expansive child and should be required reading for all who want to create space and freedom for their child of any gender to be their full, authentic self, free of enforced expectations."

—**Ellen Kahn**, senior director, Programs and Partnerships, Human Rights Campaign Foundation

"This book is a lifeline for families with transgender kids. Even more, it is like a manual, filled with stories, theology, resources, and wisdom. This is a must-read for church leaders, people of faith, and all who care about trans and nonbinary kids and their families."

—**Michael Rinehart**, bishop of the Texas-Louisiana Gulf Coast Synod, Evangelical Lutheran Church in America

"Parenting is simultaneously glorious and messy. Parents want their children to be safe, but also to flourish, and sometimes those desires don't align. Jamie Bruesehoff takes you through the hard decisions, the mistakes, and the moments of unexpected strength and clarity, all in service of providing guidance to the parents and other adults with transgender children in their lives. In this politicized environment, where transgender children and youth are under constant attack, Bruesehoff gives the reader a roadmap for listening, protecting, and clearing a path to be the person God made them to be."

—**Ross Murray**, vice president of Education & Training at the GLAAD Media Institute, founding director of The Naming Project, and author of *Made, Known, Loved: Developing LGBTQ-Inclusive Youth Ministry* and *The Everyday Advocate: Living Out Your Calling to Social Justice*

"I have been waiting and waiting for this book to exist, and now it's here! In the face of relentless attacks against the trans community, the time is yesterday for the church to speak up and out for this beautiful group of human beings. Fortunately, you now have a guide to do exactly that, in Jamie's incisive and compassionate voice."

—**Cindy Wang Brandt**, author of *Parenting Forward* and *You Are Revolutionary*

"This book fills me with hope for future generations of gender-diverse kids. Jamie Bruesehoff shares her family's story in a way that is accessible and also full of heart. Jamie's advocacy and everyday example of a mother's unconditional love will inspire and move readers in a way that's so needed. I wish I'd had this book when I was growing up—but I'm so glad it exists now."

—**Grace Baldridge (Semler)**, chart-topping Christian music artist and media host

"Jamie Bruesehoff has written an essential resource for all of us who want to be more LGBTQIA2S+ affirming. Her vulnerable writing provides a grace-filled entry point for all of us on our learning journey, no matter where we find ourselves. It is impossible to hear about her family's story and not be inspired to love all of God's children more fiercely. Give this book to the ally or skeptic in your life, and they will find the challenge and encouragement that they need. In other words, get ready to buy a lot of copies!"

—**David Scherer (AGAPE)**, performing artist and
cofounder of JUSTmoveculture.com

"Jamie Bruesehoff has written a deeply compassionate and absolutely necessary book for our time. *Raising Kids Beyond the Binary* will be grounding for Christian parents who know they love their kid but aren't sure how to set that love free to move mountains. Jamie's gentle questions, honesty, and experience will give family members of trans youth the confidence to step into a better future for us all. This is exactly the book I've been wanting to recommend to people."

—**Austen Hartke**, author of *Transforming: The Bible and
the Lives of Transgender Christians*

"Love, faith, hope, growth, and communication are the components Jamie Bruesehoff brings to life in this journey of her transgender child and family. By sharing her experiences, we witness the importance of moving beyond a place of either having a home of faith and spirituality or supporting your transgender child—to the profoundly powerful and healing place of having a home of faith, spirituality, *and* tremendous love for your transgender child. This book has truly inspired me as a care provider for transgender, gender-nonbinary, and gender-expansive children and youth to keep going and stay strong despite all that is going on in our world right now. At a time when there are hard winds and dark skies, this book offers hope, joy, and strength."

—**Linda A. Hawkins**, director, Gender & Sexuality Development Program at the Children's Hospital of Philadelphia

"'Being transgender is who God created me to be.' Rebekah Bruesehoff's simple—yet deeply profound—answer to her doctor's question is the theological and social underpinning of her mom, Jamie's book, *Raising Kids Beyond the Binary*. It is easy to make broad, sweeping generalizations and judgments until you develop a relationship with someone. In her book, Jamie opens a door and invites you into her family's story and, in doing so, creates a pathway to understanding and compassion. Jamie shares her experiences and the wisdom she's gained through them. This book should be read by anyone who works with young people. It is an important story that needs to be read and understood."

—**Todd Buegler**, senior pastor, Trinity Lutheran Church, Owatonna, Minnesota, and executive director of the ELCA Youth Ministry Network

Raising Kids beyond the Binary

# RAISING

# KIDS

# BEYOND

# THE

# BINARY

## Celebrating God's Transgender and Gender-Diverse Children

### JAMIE BRUESEHOFF

Broadleaf Books
Minneapolis

RAISING KIDS BEYOND THE BINARY
Celebrating God's Transgender and Gender-Diverse Children

Library of Congress Cataloging-in-Publication Data

Names: Bruesehoff, Jamie, author.
Title: Raising kids beyond the binary : celebrating God's transgender and gender-diverse children / Jamie Bruesehoff.
Description: Minneapolis : Broadleaf Books, [2023] | Includes bibliographical references.
Identifiers: LCCN 2023004870 (print) | LCCN 2023004871 (ebook) | ISBN 9781506488646 (hardcover) | ISBN 9781506488653 (ebook)
Subjects: LCSH: Parents of transgender children . | Transgender children. | Child rearing.
Classification: LCC HQ759.9147 .B784 2023 (print) | LCC HQ759.9147 (ebook) | DDC 649/.1564—dc23/eng/20230210
LC record available at https://lccn.loc.gov/2023004870
LC ebook record available at https://lccn.loc.gov/2023004871

Cover design: Richard Tapp

Print ISBN: 978-1-5064-8864-6
eBook ISBN: 978-1-5064-8865-3

For all those who have been told God doesn't make mistakes as if it was a bad thing, I'm so glad you were created to be you.

In memory of Leelah Alcorn

# CONTENTS

# CONTENTS

# FOREWORD

Parenting is never easy.

Even in the calmest moments, it can feel like life utterly intensified. The highs—the hopes, the achievements, and the triumphs for your child—are higher. The lows—the pain, the fear, and, tragically, sometimes the loss—that much lower. And while there is no single universal guide to every twist and turn a family may face, simply knowing that you're not alone can be life affirming for a parent and lifesaving for their child.

When I first came out to my parents as transgender, still just a junior in college, they were scared. They were fearful for my future. They envisioned a life for me filled with discrimination and rejection. They worried how our community would respond. They felt, in many ways, like they were losing me. And they were afraid that I'd never find love or fulfillment.

Whether you have a transgender child or not, all a parent wants is for their child to be happy, healthy, and safe. After I came out, my parents simply needed to know that such a hope was still possible and that a path existed for their out trans child to find love, be loved, and do work that I love in a community I love.

It was 2011, more than a year before Laverne Cox graced *Time Magazine*'s cover under the headline "The Transgender

Tipping Point." Their fears were rooted in the same reality that my fears were rooted in; there were not many examples of transgender people who were out and reaching their dreams.

My parents' first step in their search for support was to reach out to the pastors at our family church, a Presbyterian congregation that I was raised in and where my parents forged deep friendships. While our pastors, like my parents, were clearly trying to grapple with a topic that was largely unknown to them, their instinct was right: to listen and to love.

Through our pastors and essentially a trans-version of *Six Degrees of Kevin Bacon*, our church's leaders were able to connect my parents with the only people who could instill in them some level of hope that things would be okay. They were connected to another couple with a transgender child.

Even before talking with them, simply being connected with another family who had gone through something similar made a world of difference. They were not alone.

Eventually, after talking with those parents and dozens of others they were connected with, they were able to walk beside me, first hesitantly and eventually with unmitigated pride, as I became my authentic self.

Fast forward more than a decade later and the world looks very different than it did when I came out. While transgender people still much demonized, most people have some conception of what it means to be transgender. Trans people can look to examples of out and proud trans actors and artists, entrepreneurs, and elected officials. Trans young people have peers like Rebekah Bruesehoff that they can look up to. Parents have visible examples of loving and affirming parents like Jamie Bruesehoff.

Whether you are opening this book as a parent of a transgender young person or a curious reader hoping to understand more about the beautiful diversity of our society, this book will provide you with a path forward. Parents will find comfort and guidance. Allies will be empowered. All readers will gain the privilege of a beautiful story of a family that embodies love in its deepest, most grace-filled form.

The Bruesehoff family reflects how far we've come. They embody the idea that identities too often viewed in conflict—being both people of faith and an LGBTQ family—actually complement one another. Indeed, the values of love and grace are at the heart of both. Rebekah, a young, smart, and vibrant transgender teen, lives a life that would have seemed impossible to me as a kid by both living her truth and dreaming big dreams all at the same time.

Families like the Bruesehoffs personify our progress.

Unfortunately, at this particularly toxic moment for the trans community, trans young people and their parents have found themselves at the center of a cruel and concerted political attack. Politicians are attempting to criminalize loving and supporting your child if they happen to be transgender. They are pursuing bans on gender affirming care in what amounts to government-mandated conversion therapy through physical and mental torture. To put it bluntly, disingenuous and dangerous politicians are trying to eliminate young people like Rebekah from our society.

For trans people—especially trans young people—the stakes could not be higher.

And that's why books like this one are so important. We need positive examples of families like the Bruesehoffs who show that having a transgender child is not a failure of parenting. We need to show that God's heart is big enough for all of us and that loving God and loving a transgender child go hand-in-hand. We need to see that when trans young people are loved and embraced, they can flourish in spite of the challenges that society puts in our way. And we need to provide hope to trans kids and their families that it can be okay.

Trans people deserve life. We deserve love. And we deserve hope.

In January 2020, when I was sworn in as the nation's first openly transgender state senator and highest ranking openly transgender elected official in the country, I asked Rebekah to hold my Bible. As I stood there next to my own parents and took my oath to protect and defend the Constitutions that make our liberty possible, I looked at Rebekah. And I felt hope.

With loving families like the Bruesehoffs, the future is bright. Now, as they invite you in on their journey, I know you will find hope, too.

—*Senator Sarah McBride*

# INTRODUCTION

Church was the only place where I ever told my child that she could not be her true self. My oldest child, Rebekah, is transgender. When she was born, we all thought she was a boy, but she deeply knows herself to be a girl. Before the word *transgender* ever crossed our minds, we knew Rebekah didn't fit into society's box labeled "boy." From the time she was two years old, Rebekah loved all things pink, purple, and sparkly. Rainbows and glitter mesmerized her. She loved to put flowery clips in her hair and play dress up. I didn't necessarily care if she had pink toys, but I did have practical concerns. What if we bought her all the pink things? Would she one day wake up and hate pink, like most boys? Then what would we do? I couldn't afford to replace it all. Putting aside any potential financial implications and following her lead, the mantra in our family became: Colors are for everyone. Clothes are for everyone. You can be any kind of boy you want to be.

Eventually, we learned terms like *gender nonconforming*, *gender expansive*, and, our favorite, coined by Dr. Diane Ehrensaft,[1] *gender creative*. These were the words psychologists used when they talked about kids like ours, kids who reject stereotypes and societal expectations around gender roles. At three years old, Rebekah loved playing pretend salon and painting each other's nails, an admittedly messy endeavor. In kindergarten, her school notebooks were covered in hearts and peace signs. When she turned seven, she wanted to go shopping and pick out her own clothes, but there weren't any in colors she liked in the boys' section. Together, we braved the girls' section of Target. I'd never seen her happier as she ooh-ed and ahh-ed over all the options, completely oblivious to people's stares.

We were navigating the murky territory of supporting our outside-of-the-box kid in a shove-you-in-a-box kind of world. Every time my husband and I had the conversation, the outcome was the same. The world may not be kind. People may not understand. However, letting our child unapologetically show up as themselves in the world was how God called us to parent. It was always a yes—to the nails, the shoes, the dance classes, the clothes. Yes. Be any kind of boy you want to be.

It was always a yes until Easter 2015. This time was different. She was eight years old, and this was the first time she'd asked to wear a dress besides the play clothes in the dress-up bin. She wanted to wear a dress to church on Easter Sunday. If you're a churchgoer, then you know Easter is kind of a big deal. In fact, it's such a big deal that it brings out many people who haven't been to church since Christmas. Don't get me wrong, I have no problem with those folks. Growing up, my family were those folks. But it did impact my child's request. There were going to be a lot of extra people at church who didn't know our family nearly as well as the Sunday regulars.

This is the part where I should explain I am married to a Lutheran pastor. My spouse is a pastor in the Evangelical Lutheran Church in America (ELCA). At the time, he was the pastor of a small congregation in a rural, conservative part of New Jersey. Rural and conservative in New Jersey may not mean what it means elsewhere, but we did have cows in our backyard. While our congregation had quietly supported or at least gotten used to our child's gender nonconformity, we did not know how they would respond if our eight-year-old child, whom they knew as a boy, showed up in a frilly Easter dress. We did not know if we would be able to keep our child safe, how to navigate questions, how to run interference on such a busy, stressful, crowded Sunday.

So we said no. We said we know this is who you are, we see you and we love you, but we just need you to wait. The message we sent to our child was that being who you are at church is scary, and we needed her to pretend to be someone else a little longer. I cannot tell that story or write those words without my stomach churning. I grieve that *no*. I also know we were doing the best we could at the time, and I can have grace for that. What bothers me the most is that I don't know, if I could go back and do it again, if I would do it any differently. We weren't wrong. Being a transgender or gender-diverse person at church was scary. It's still scary.

I grieve a lot from that time. I grieve that we spent eight years of my child's life not knowing who she was. I grieve that she had to go through so much pain for us all to figure it out. I grieve that she is living in a world that isn't ready for her, a world where people like her are rejected, bullied, harassed, hurt, and killed just because of their identity. I grieve that in the years since that Easter, since she transitioned, she has spent so much time speaking up for inclusion and for her community. There is grief mixed with my pride every time I watch her share her story or speak with legislators. She's incredible, but no child should have to spend their time defending their existence and teaching others how to make space for them.

Perhaps most of all, I grieve that showing up in the church fully as herself was one of the hardest parts of her transition for her, for our family. It's not because our congregation was full of terrible people. They are good people—kind, smart, compassionate, and loving—but even good people can do harm by the things they do and those they fail to do. We also cannot ignore that the wider church, the Christian church, has a deeply contentious relationship with transgender people, and Christians continue to do the loudest, most significant damage to the trans and nonbinary communities, personally and politically.

Rebekah did show up at church as herself a few weeks after Easter and every week after that. It was scary and hard. It was also beautiful and life giving. That first Sunday, I sat in the pew with Rebekah and her siblings. She proudly wore a purple dress adorned with tulle and flowers. I struggled to steady my breathing while my heart tried to jump out of my chest. I went through the motions. Stand up, sit down, sing the songs. As we turned to share the peace, I plastered a smile on my face, shaking hands and praying no one would say anything. *Peace be with you.* By the time worship was over, I was ready to make a run for it. I needed to get out. I needed fresh air. That's when I saw him. My husband was shaking hands with people as they left the sanctuary like he did every Sunday, and one particular member was headed his way. I could tell this man had something to say. He always had something to say—whether it was in church or on Facebook.

He said, "Listen, I don't understand this whole transgender thing." I watched my husband brace himself for what was coming. The man continued, "But she used to hide behind your wife and not answer me when I said hi. And today? Today, she ran up to me, twirled in her dress, and gave me a high-five." He shrugged. "What more is there to know?"

That's the good news. We, as parents and as the church, don't have to have this all figured out. We won't always understand. We have to learn and do the work, but no one is asking for perfection here. We're going to mess up. We're going to use the wrong words. However, we can be clear that transgender and gender-expansive children are whole and holy. They are not mistakes; they are who God created them to be, and the body of Christ is more fully present when they are here with us.

That's why I wrote this book. That's why I work with families, congregations, camps, and denominations all over the country to create safer and more welcoming spaces for these kids. They need you, and the church needs them. Wouldn't it be amazing if every little Rebekah, every family, knew that at your church, every young person would be safe, loved, and celebrated in the fullness of their identity—whatever that identity may be?

The chapters that follow are anchored by my own family's story. I will share my experience as a mother walking with and learning from my own transgender child as well as working with hundreds of families across the country doing the same. This book will equip you to journey alongside families raising transgender and gender-diverse children and youth. Maybe you're a parent to one of these young people, or maybe you're a pastor wondering how your church can show up for them. Together, we'll explore what it means and what it looks like to create space for these gender-expansive young people in our lives and our faith communities.

Before we begin, I need to start by naming the place of transgender elders in our story and our life. Rebekah could not be who she is, in the church or the world, without the transgender and nonbinary people, especially Black and brown transgender women, who came before her and relentlessly instigated change. Sylvia Rivera, Marsha P. Johnson, Gloria Allen (better known as Mama Gloria), Monica Helms, Barbara "Babs" Siperstein, and Monica Roberts are just some of the trailblazers whose lives and work changed the course of history and changed what was possible for families like mine. In the face of harassment, discrimination, systemic oppression, and horrific violence, they paved the way with their courage, their visibility, and their fight for a world radically different from the one in which they lived.

Beyond my own daughter, these transgender elders have been my greatest teachers. Whether through hearing their stories shared by those who knew them, reading about them in books, or actually being in relationship with them, they've taught me how to better show up for my child and how to be an accomplice in the work of not only her liberation but the liberation of all people. They've radically changed the way I see the world. And those with whom I've been honored to be in community have spoken words of grace and life into me in a way I've never deserved. Not only have these elders paved the way for children like mine, but they continue to be our children's most ardent advocates and fiercest protectors.

And I'm still learning. As a white cisgender woman (that is, a woman who is not transgender), my worldview is steeped in privilege and informed by my own lived experience. I'll write more about this later, but it is critical that you as a reader know my limitations and intentions. I continue to learn from transgender and nonbinary people. I continue to learn from Black people,

Indigenous people, and people of color. It is my earnest hope that the chapters that follow honor the work and wisdom of their voices and lives, and I know I will spend the rest of my life learning how to do that better.

One more important note: When Rebekah was born, we described her as a boy. We used male pronouns and a traditionally masculine name we chose before she was born. We did this until Rebekah socially transitioned at eight years old—that meant we changed her name and pronouns so she could go out in the world as herself. Rebekah is now sixteen. In this book, whether I am describing her before or after her transition, I will only use female pronouns and what we describe as her "forever name." She is a girl named Rebekah, and any words we used to describe her before were simply placeholders. Also, I share everything that I share with her explicit permission. While the stories I share are told from my perspective and rooted in my experience, they cannot be fully extracted from her story, and she has complete authority over that.

Two years after that Easter when we said no, two years after Rebekah transitioned, we gathered with our congregation, our family, and Rebekah's godparents, and we celebrated and blessed her and her forever name. In that service, we prayed, "O God, in renaming your servants Abraham, Sarah, Jacob, Peter, and Paul, you gave them new lives and new tasks, new love and new hope. We now hold before you your child, Rebekah Eleanor."

This is what it can look like for an imperfect church to welcome, love, and celebrate a child for who they are, who God made them to be. What does this look like for you? For your family? For your specific place of ministry? I will give you the tools to answer those questions.

Raising a gender-diverse child has meant learning all sorts of practical things about transgender people in the world and what it means to be welcoming and inclusive. Most of all, Rebekah has taught us what it means to love the person in front of you, not for who you thought they were or wished they would be but for who they know themselves to be. She showed us what it looks like to advocate for yourself and others. And she made real to us what it means to be the body of Christ in the world. Now more than ever, the church and the world need these lessons of love, grace, courage, and hope. So let's get started.

# 1 | RAISING MY RAINBOW

In 2007, my spouse and I gave birth to our first child, a child we thought was a boy but who we now know to be a girl. This child came out of the womb demanding her voice be heard, or no one was going to sleep again. She screamed for hours on end and slept for only twenty minutes at a time. We read all the books. We bought all the gadgets. White noise machines, eight different kinds of swaddle blankets, gripe water, gas drops, co-sleeping contraptions that kept her close to us and put her on an incline in case she had reflux. If it existed in 2007, we tried it. There seemed to be no explanation and no solution. She was colicky.

There was nothing else we could do. So we took turns shushing, rocking, walking, and bouncing, and we prayed to make it to the three-month mark, when we were told colic would resolve itself. Except three months came and went, and life didn't get easier. She was a "high needs" child. We gave up on finding a solution in a book or a store, and we just followed her lead. If something calmed her, we did it. And if nothing calmed her, we held her and loved her while she cried. One time after a particularly rough day, I called our pediatrician and asked why she could possibly still be crying. He said, "I don't know. Maybe she's a Yankees fan." As a desperate new mom, it was the last thing I wanted to hear, but it affirmed for me that sometimes things aren't going to make sense, and all we can do is love our kids through it. In time the constant crying stopped, and eventually we slept through the night.

It was baptism by fire as far as parenting went, and it taught us some very important lessons early on. Everyone wanted to tell us what our kid needed—family, neighbors, church members, strangers in the checkout line at the grocery store—and they were wrong every time. The only thing that got our little family of three through was getting to know this baby, listening to her, and trusting her to show us the next right thing to do. That was the foundation for our parenting journey. This tiny human in our arms knew herself better than we could ever know her, better than any book or parenting expert could know her. Our job was to listen and follow her lead. So we did.

It was an adventure from the start. She was an early crawler, an early walker, and an early talker. She climbed on everything and explored everywhere. She was the kind of kid who broke her arm at fifteen months old. We called the pediatrician because she had fallen earlier in the day and wouldn't use her arm or put any weight on it. He sent us for an x-ray just before offices closed on Friday. It was broken. Of course, it was now Friday night, every parent's favorite time for a medical emergency. She needed it stabilized, and that meant we were going to the emergency room. We told the triage nurse that our toddler had a broken arm. She looked at us kindly, if a little condescendingly, and said, "Oh, don't worry. Their bones are quite flexible at this age; they don't usually break." We handed her the x-ray. "Oh."

So often we treat new parents like we do children. We assume we know so much more than they do, and that teaches them to doubt themselves. If there was one thing I could offer to new parents, it would not necessarily be a piece of advice but maybe an affirmation. You know yourself. You know your baby. Together, you will get to know each other even more. Get quiet. Listen. Trust yourself and trust them. Humans who are loved, supported, heard, and allowed to lead themselves don't end up spoiled. They end up deeply grounded and beautifully empowered. That will carry you from infancy through the teenage years. Or at least it has carried us this far.

In many ways, that's what this book is about. Beyond our ideas of gender diversity and identity, this is about learning how to raise children who are able to step into the fullness of who God created them to be every step of the way. And I think, if we're lucky, along the way we raise ourselves into being able to do the same.

## COLORS ARE FOR EVERYONE

Rebekah was two and a half years old when she saw a princess Halloween costume during a rare trip to the mall. She immediately asked if she could have it. I told her we weren't shopping for Halloween right then and steered her in another direction. She didn't ask again. She dressed up as a lion that year as part of a trio, with her cousin dressed as a tiger and her brother dressed as a bear. Lions, tigers, and bears! And you can be sure the grownups dressed in homemade T-shirts that read "Oh my!" Yes, it was corny but fun.

But why? Why didn't I just say yes to the princess costume? I mean, there were practical reasons. We weren't shopping for Halloween costumes that day. Just like I didn't want to have to replace all her toys when she suddenly woke up one day hating pink. Practical, sure. But it was also easy. Easy because she was little, and she didn't mind. Easy in that I didn't have to figure out how to deal with having a child we believed was a boy dressed up like a princess on Halloween. If she had pushed, if she had asked repeatedly, we would have made it work. But instead, I gently steered her into what society told us she was *supposed* to want to be and hoped that was that.

For quite some time, I struggled with where to draw the line. Was I allowing her to make her own decisions without forcing societal norms on her? Pink. Sparkles. Fairies. When she outright asked for that stuff, I didn't say no. She could have the pink stuff. We owned fairy and princess movies, and we watched them often. I assured myself I wasn't one of *those* parents. You know the ones. The ones who will only let their boys play with trucks, dinosaurs, and "boy stuff," whatever that means. Family members commented when we got her a kitchen for her second birthday or when they saw her playing with a pink doll stroller that we got from our local freecycle group. They weren't being rude or mean; they were just surprised. A kitchen for a boy? A pink stroller? Of course, because little boys can cook and take care of babies just like grown men can. See, I wasn't one of *those* people. We were progressive. Open-minded.

But the more I reflected, the more I wondered if maybe I wasn't as open-minded as I thought. When I was at the store looking at something to buy for her, I'd consider the options. If there was a blue water bottle with dinosaurs (she did love dinosaurs) and a pink water bottle with Tinkerbell (she also loved Tinkerbell), which did I buy? The dinosaurs. Why? Because that's what the world around me was telling me I was supposed to do. Because it was easier. Maybe she would have liked that

Tinkerbell one more. Maybe I should have bought it. But at the time, she was pretty darn happy with dinosaurs because she didn't know Tinkerbell was an option.

Every purchase became a huge decision. I hoped the fact that we were aware enough to care and open enough to love our kid whoever she ended up being meant we weren't screwing up entirely. She was three years old when she first asked for a pink shirt. I combed the thrift store racks trying to find something that didn't have ruffles or lace, finally landing on a bold pink T-shirt with the PowerPuff Girls on the front and just a little bit of glitter. She loved that shirt. She wore it for years and years, as often as possible. A few weeks later, I found some purple pajamas covered in flowers. Pajamas, perfect! No one would need to see them besides us. She wore those until they fell apart. It took some time, but eventually we decided pink was just a color. And even if it was more than a color, even if it was some indicator of who she might someday be, we were okay with that. Of course, we had no idea she could be transgender; we barely knew the word outside of daytime talk shows and tabloids. We assumed, if anything, that she'd be gay.

That same year, she was given the role of a bird in the preschool play. She was adamant that she wanted to be a pink bird. I took a deep breath, thought tropical, and went for it. Money was tight, so I visited our local big-box store. I came home with a pair of pink leggings two sizes too small on clearance, some pink satin fabric I found in a bargain bin, a stack of colorful craft foam sheets, a foam visor, and a can of spray adhesive. This level of crafting was way beyond my capabilities. I just wasn't that kind of mom. But if my kid wanted to be a pink bird, I would make it happen. My husband helped. We used staples (yes, staples) and iron-on hem tape to form the pink satiny fabric into a tunic. We cut the craft foam into feather shapes and used the spray adhesive to stick it to the tunic. We repurposed the foam visor as a beak, covered her sneakers with some tall yellow socks to look like bird legs, cut the leggings so the ragged bottoms looked a little like leg feathers, and topped it all off with some pink hair spray from the party store.

It was a sight to behold, in a ridiculous way. But Rebekah was thrilled. Standing there in this costume held together by spray adhesive and staples, she grinned at us. That grin was all we needed to know we had done well. Later that day, we sat in the pews of the church where the preschool play was happening, camera in hand, ready to capture our little one's stage debut in *The Little Mermaid*. The birds made their entrance. My jaw dropped. My hand flew to my mouth to hide my surprise. We had made a mistake. I didn't know whether to laugh or cry. These birds were seagulls. There stood our bright-pink little Rebekah, glowing with excitement, next to all the children in their gray and white. Honestly, it fit her perfectly.

## "ANYTHING BUT PINK AND PURPLE"

Of course, the people around us had opinions about her daily choices. Kids at preschool would ask why she was wearing a pink shirt. They'd tell her pink was for girls. They'd ask why her nails were painted. Her preschool teachers were perplexed. They suggested that maybe we just stop painting her nails, "you know, to avoid the confusion." Instead, we taught Rebekah (and her teachers) that colors and clothes are for everyone. We told Rebekah, "You can be any kind of boy you want to be." We had no idea she wasn't a boy. We were still learning, but in giving her the language to respond to people's questions, we were solidifying our own beliefs about the gender expectations society puts on us all. We were learning in real time how to love and support this pink and sparkly kid, who spent her days going from elaborate train track setups to twirling in my old dance recital costumes, from lovingly caring for her baby dolls to building the most elaborate Lego worlds, where her toy dinosaurs roamed.

She didn't like kids asking her questions. She began to notice the looks adults gave her. Shortly after her fifth birthday, she declared that pink and purple were not her favorite colors anymore. What were her new favorites? "Anything but pink and purple." She still played with her pink toys. She'd wear her purple pajamas, but she no longer reached for the pink shirt when leaving the house. She completely stopped asking for new pink and purple things.

Then one day, I found out why. She didn't want to go to school. She didn't want to go to school because the boys at school didn't believe her when she told them her favorite colors were anything except pink and purple. She didn't want to go to school because when she said her favorite colors were anything except pink and purple, they whispered to each other that they knew she really *did* like pink and purple.

My heart broke. My heart broke because I could not protect her from this. My heart broke because my child, who liked pink all on her own and who proudly continued to like pink even though she knew some people thought she shouldn't, was now trying to hide what she liked to avoid being teased. And despite her best efforts, she was still being teased. My heart broke because the parents of these boys didn't teach them that pink is just a color, and my child was the one who had to deal with that.

My heart broke because I hadn't been able to give her enough love, support, and confidence to just keep liking pink. My love wasn't enough in the face of the world.

I wanted to hug her and shake her. I wanted to call those boys nasty names and tell my child to like whatever colors she actually liked. I wanted to tell her there are dumb parents in the world who raise mean kids. But instead, forcing myself to stay calm, I asked, "How does that make you feel?"

She poked at the eggs on her breakfast plate and without looking at me said, "Sad."

Deep breath. "It's not nice for those boys to hurt your feelings. You can like any color you want. Pink is just a color." She took a bite and didn't respond, so I kept going. "They shouldn't whisper about you. That's not okay, and that's not your fault."

She looked up at me with tears filling her eyes. I pulled her onto my lap and hugged her tight. I wanted to make it all better, and I knew I couldn't. Instead, I reminded her that it was good to ask a teacher for help if someone was hurting her feelings, even though I knew she wouldn't. She was my sensitive little one who internalized things and talked about them weeks or even months later. She wasn't going to say anything. This terrified me.

Then I sent her off to school. I sent her off to school, where she worked with, played with, and ate lunch with those boys like she always did. I picked her up at the end of the day, and she asked when she could have her next playdate with them. After all that, they were her friends. I wanted to yell at them for making her feel bad and yell at their parents for not teaching their sons better. I needed them all to do better, to *be* better.

I couldn't protect her. I still can't. The only thing I can do is assure her that she is wonderful just the way she is. I can make sure she knows she is loved and accepted unconditionally by the people close to her. I can listen, managing my own rage, my fear, and my hurt so that she feels safe talking. And I can model how we treat others, being careful with my words and my opinions, so that she knows it's never okay to make fun of someone. It's never okay to hurt someone's feelings or say things that could hurt someone's feelings if they heard them. Isn't that something we could all be reminded of occasionally? This parenting stuff never gets easier.

These days, thanks in part to progress made by queer people and LGBTQ+ advocates in breaking down the gender boxes, and in part thanks to social media, there are visible examples of kids living in a way not limited by the gender binary, crossing the divide between the pink and blue toy aisles, and proudly being themselves even when it doesn't fit our culture's tiny view of what it means to be a boy or a girl. Stores have begun to offer gender-neutral clothing lines, and public figures proudly model what it looks like to reject the gender binary in expression and/or identity. My experience raising a young gender-nonconforming child will sound archaic to some, while in other communities, it will be revolutionary.

## EVERYONE HAS A GENDER JOURNEY

Gender impacts us all, and if we're going to raise young people who are confident in and capable of expressing their gender in ways that are truest to themselves, we must take a good look at the world around us. Each one of us has a gender journey. I can think back to occasions when I was treated differently because I was a girl. There were times when boys were complimented on their strength and intelligence, while people told me I was pretty or cute. I can remember crying in dressing rooms as young as ten years old. I hated dresses, but my mom wanted me to find clothing that was appropriate for whatever event we were attending. Pantsuits weren't a thing for little girls then. Like most women, I've spent my life being told I am either too feminine or not feminine enough. When I showed leadership, I was told I was bossy. When my teachers needed volunteers to help carry something heavy, my flailing hand in the air was ignored while my boy classmates were chosen. Even as an adult, I once sat in the ER having an anaphylactic allergic reaction (to watermelon, making summer barbeques thereafter a little less sweet), struggling to breathe, and I was told by a medical professional to stop being so dramatic. Meanwhile, men are taught to hide their emotions, avoid any indications of weakness, and succeed at all costs.

We can speak about the way gender impacts people in generalities, and there's plenty of data to support that, but I want you to go a step further and consider how gender has impacted you specifically. What are the things you weren't allowed to do because of who the world said you were? When were the times you stepped out of that box, and how did that impact you and the people around you? How did the beliefs and expectations of your family of origin or cultural background inform how you felt about your gender? My experience of gender as a white woman has likely been different from that of a Black woman or an Asian woman, for example. Were you ever misgendered in person, in print, or on the phone? How did that feel? With a name like Jamie, people have often assumed I'm a boy before they met me. Sometimes that felt freeing, and other times that felt shameful. By taking the time to delve into how gender has impacted us, we can be better prepared for and aware of what it's going to mean to raise the child in front of us in a pervasively gendered world.

It's not easy to raise outside-of-the-box kids in a shove-you-in-a-box kind of world. It requires us to get honest about our personal expectations and baggage around gender, as well as the expectations and baggage of the world around us. When someone sees their little boy in a dress for the first time, they may have some feelings. And when he goes to the grocery store in that dress for the first time, they're going to have some more feelings. And when he wants to go to church in that dress for the first time, there will probably be even more feelings. We will be challenged to unpack our own personal reactions, and then we will be challenged to navigate our fear for his safety and his well-being. The same can be true when a little girl cuts her long hair short or when she wears a suit and tie instead of a frilly dress for a special occasion. How do we allow our children to be their freest selves in a world that won't always be kind? How do we send our children off to school knowing there are kids teasing them for their favorite colors? And what do we do when the world tries to change our children right before our very eyes?

## WHAT THE WORLD THINKS

There are two sides to this coin. First, we deal with what the world will think of us. Then we deal with what the world will think of our children. No matter how progressive and evolved we may believe ourselves to be, the world's opinion of us usually carries more weight than we'd like. This is especially true for mothers, who face relentless scrutiny and judgment around parenting. Breast or bottle feed? Cry it out or gentle parenting? Homeschool or public school? If you're a working mom, you clearly don't care about your children. If you're a stay-at-home mom, you are lazy and indulgent. Society regularly blames mothers for whatever they believe to be "wrong" about a child. I know I'm frequently blamed for having a transgender child, whether in comments on social media, emails, articles written about me, and occasionally even to my face. People explain that if I had just not given her toys from the "girl" aisle, she wouldn't be trans. They tell me, and everyone watching, how it was the food dye and the GMOs that I fed her (ironically, she was raised dye-free and on organic food for the first decade of her life). They will explain how it's all because I wanted a daughter and didn't get one that I made my son be the little girl for which I hoped or how I didn't want a gay son, so I made her transgender. They accuse me of Munchausen by proxy over and over again.

If you are wrapped up in what the world will think of you, you're not going to be able to hold space for your child to be themselves in the way they will need. So let's get this out of the way. What does it say about you that your child doesn't fit in a box? What does it say about you that your little boy loves to twirl and whirl in a princess gown or your little girl wants a short hair-cut and to wear a tie instead of a skirt? Some will say it means you're indulgent; you will let your child do anything they want. Is that true? Does your child stay up all hours of the night because they want to? Do you let them eat cotton candy three meals a day for weeks at a time? Do you let them hit their friends and bite their siblings? My guess is the answer is no on all counts.

Others will say it means you reject the teachings of the Bible, and you're leading your child astray. Is that true? While I can't speak to your own connection to the teachings of the Bible, I can say wholeheartedly that allowing your child to be themselves, whatever that may look like, is not leading them away from the God who created them. We'll dig deeper into this later, but conflating Jesus's teachings with the standards and expectations of the dominant culture of our time or of Jesus's time is not only inaccurate; it's dangerous. It puts God into a box of our own making, of our own deciding. God is so much bigger than that. It's also in direct opposition to who Jesus was in his time on earth. He regularly questioned and rejected the cultural and religious norms of his day. He actively sought to dismantle systems of power and oppression. Jesus broke down boxes and shattered binaries, and I'm going to take a strong guess that he doesn't care if your little boy's nails are painted pink, purple, or any other color.

Still others will suggest you're giving in to peer pressure, that you've fallen prey to some liberal agenda. Is that the case? Has your child's refusal to fit into the gendered boxes that some of their peers feel so comfortable in come from you? From the world? Did you force them to only play with toys that aren't typically gendered and to dress in clothing that is not what's expected of them based on the sex they were assigned at birth? In all my work, in the hundreds of parents of transgender and gender-nonconforming children with whom I've been honored to connect, I have yet to meet the parent who answers yes to any of these questions. Maybe they gave their child access to all kinds of toys, books, and colors, but never have I met a parent who forced their child to only engage in gender-nonconforming behavior. If that's you, it's probably time to reach out to a professional for support on this parenting journey. I trust you're doing the best you can, and we all need support sometimes. If that's not you, then name and claim that so when others try to say it about you, you know deep in your being that it's simply not true. Keep in mind, the world will say different things about us based on the places we live, the families we come from, the cultures we navigate, and the colors of our skin.

So what does it actually say about you that you have a child who lives somewhat or entirely outside the binary gender expectations of our time? You may not be sure just yet, and that's okay. This is what it tells me. It tells me you're raising a human brave enough to be themselves while the world tells them they should be someone else. Sometimes our small humans are resilient, courageous, and wise despite us as parents; I don't think we can or should take credit for their greatness. At the same time, when I see a parent striving to love, support, and encourage their out-of-the-box child, I see a love strong enough and bold enough to do really hard things. I see parents who are refusing to get in the way of their child's wellness and wholeness. I see parents who are parenting themselves first so they can better parent their child.

It took some time for me to get over what the world was going to think of me when Rebekah showed up in pink and sparkles, but I got there. Unfortunately, I never got over worrying what the world was going to do to her when she showed up as herself. It was one thing to manage that fear, to put on my happy face and project confidence for her so she could be confident, but it was another to walk the fine line of deciding if and how to prepare her for the potential lack of understanding from those around her. I hear it from parents all the time. How do I support my child in being the truest version of themselves and still protect them from the jerks and bullies of the world? (To be honest, they usually use much more colorful language than *jerks* and *bullies*.)

Or sometimes we flip it. How do we protect our kids from, ahem, *jerks and bullies* and not also make our children feel shame around expressing themselves?

## THE BEST PATH FORWARD

Helping our children negotiate their own preferences versus the anticipated reactions of the people around them (and the potential safety concerns that come with those people) is not simple or easy. In a utopia, children could wear what they want and like what they like without repercussions, but that's not our reality. Sometimes our children will come to us with their concerns about how people have treated or will treat them based on their choices. Other times, our children are blissfully unaware, and we must decide whether to warn them of what might happen. I find most people's initial reactions are one of two extremes. On one hand, we want to tell them not to wear or do that thing because we don't want the big, bad, scary world to hurt them. Period. End of discussion. Alternatively, we want to tell them to wear the clothes, do the thing, be themselves no matter what the world says or does. We don't want to see our children cave under the pressures of the people around them for all the reasons it broke my heart when my daughter decided she didn't like pink or purple anymore. Like most answers in life and certainly in parenting, the best path forward is messier and more nuanced than our initial reactions suggest.

While raising confident young people who are true to themselves is always our goal, it coincides with raising young people who can listen to and trust themselves, setting boundaries and doing things on their own terms. The biggest gifts we can give them are autonomy and self-trust. That means helping them consider all the possibilities, encouraging them to listen deeply to their own intuition, to their own comfort level, to their own needs, and then empowering them to decide how best to proceed.

When your child is in the blissfully unaware category, more of this responsibility falls on you. You need to decide how much to prepare them for or not. This will vary based on your kiddo (their age, their maturity, and their temperament) as well as the situation itself. If your child is heading into a situation where you won't be able to run interference or offer any protection or respite, you're going to have different conversations than if you're accompanying your child to a location where you'll be able to pull them aside, offer support, and troubleshoot alongside them.

As parents, we must consider safety. But what does that mean? There is emotional safety, physical safety, and spiritual safety. There are places in this country that are simply not safe—emotionally, physically, or spiritually—for a child stepping outside of gender expectations. Sometimes the answer is simply that your child doesn't belong in any place or situation where they are not safe being themselves. Other times, the situation is harder to avoid, and you'll need to talk through strategies and possible solutions. These decisions will be more complex and more challenging for families who already fear for their children in a world that often meets them with trauma and violence: Black, brown, and Indigenous children; neurodiverse children; children who aren't citizens of the country where they live; and children whose primary language is not English, for example. I don't have the answers, but these are some questions and strategies to consider.

Before you have any conversation with your child about outcomes or reactions to their expression they haven't yet considered,

I implore you to get quiet and check in with yourself. Are you overwhelmed with fear? Are your fears rooted in reality or anxiety? Is there someone you can talk to for your own support before you try to support your child? While preparing your child for what lies ahead is a necessary part of parenting, it's easy to dump our fears and emotional baggage on them.

I like to use a lot of open-ended questions in talking children through scenarios and decisions. I might ask my child things like: How will you feel if you wear that? How do you feel when you wear that at home versus at school? What do you think about those feelings? What can you do if you don't like those feelings? What might it be like if someone makes a negative comment about your painted nails? How will it feel? How could you respond? What will you do if you don't feel safe? These kinds of questions lead to productive conversations while letting the child lead the way.

Role-playing can also help. Practice responses to possible comments, questions, or concerns. When we aren't prepared, even comments that aren't necessarily mean spirited can have a negative impact. Questions like "Why do you like pink so much if you're a boy?" or "Why is your hair so short if you're a girl?" are common. We can practice answers to these questions with our children to grow their confidence and equip them for a world that won't always understand their choices. Some of my favorite answers are as simple as "It's just what I like" or "Colors are for everyone."

Young gender-nonconforming children often have a specific article of clothing that makes them feel safe and secure, and they want to wear this piece of clothing all day, every day, to all places. Sometimes this could be a costume out of their dress-up bin, or other times it's a favorite pair of pajamas. Whatever it is, it's likely not appropriate for all situations. Now, when I say *appropriate*, I don't mean that it does or doesn't fit into polite society. My kids were known to show up at church on Sunday in superhero capes and bunny ears. What I mean by appropriate is whether it is safe and effective for the activity.

To consider this, I ask questions like: Can you do what you want in this clothing? Will you be able to run? Jump? Twirl? Play with friends? Will you be concerned about getting it dirty in a way that will take away from your experience? Will you have to adjust it or modify your movements so that it stays in place? I regularly use these questions with my kids regardless of their gender expression. It helps them consider if something is appropriate for the weather or if they might want to have something that covers more of their skin while steering clear of problematic (and often shaming) implications around modesty. I'll ask my teenagers if they can sit in class all day comfortably. Will they be warm enough? Cool enough? Do they have a way to adjust their outfit if they aren't? If not, maybe add a layer.

We also talk about appropriate attire for different places and occasions. While some dress codes and expectations around wardrobe can be rooted in problematic cultural or societal norms, misogyny, and white supremacy, other times dress codes or expectations help us communicate respect or appreciation. Still other times, clothing choices can help create a sense of belonging or unity. We don't really know the best path forward in a particular situation until we examine these expectations with the new lens of freedom from unnecessary restriction. All these questions and conversations help our children learn how to listen to themselves, know themselves, and make decisions that are best for them.

Sometimes the result of all these conversations and considerations will be that our child decides not to wear the dress or do the thing. They will decide they are not comfortable or ready to share that part of themselves in that place at that time. While it may pain us, this is not failure. It is a success that they have made this decision on their own terms. They do not owe the fullness of their identity or that piece of themselves to anyone. When you support them wholeheartedly in making this decision, you are showing them that you trust them to be the authority on their body and their life, which helps deepen their trust in themselves. That kind of inner trust is something most adults I know are still working to identify and grow.

## NO MATTER WHAT

That night after I'd sent Rebekah to school knowing she was being teased, I tucked her into bed, and she begged for extra snuggles. I climbed in alongside her, and with her head on my chest and my arm tucked beneath her, I whispered,

> *I love you. I will always love you. You never need to do anything to get my love. It's always here. No matter what. I will love you if you break all the rules and don't listen to anything I ask you to do. I will love you if you jump on the couch and don't go to sleep.*

She giggled, and I kept going.

> *I will love you the same whether you help with chores or eat all your dinner. I love you on good days and bad days. I love you when you are happy and sad, when you are angry or upset. I love you when I am happy and when I am sad, when I am angry and when I am upset. I*

*love you absolutely no matter what. I love you if your favorite color is yellow, pink, or blue. I will love you if you grow up to be the president of the United States, and I will love you if you never have a job in your life. I love you simply because you are exactly who you are—yesterday, today, and tomorrow. There is nothing you can do to make me love you more or less.*

*And you know what's cool, little one? The same goes for Daddy. He loves you the same way. And you know what's even cooler, my love? The same goes for God. God loves us no matter what simply because we are God's children. We have good days and bad days. Sometimes we get upset or do unkind things. We love each other and forgive each other, and God loves and forgives us. It's pretty special. There's nothing we can say or do to change any of that.*

She listened, smiling and snuggling. When I was done rambling, she snuggled in closer and asked, "Mommy, can I snuggle you all day tomorrow?" Sure, kiddo, there will be plenty of time for snuggling tomorrow. I might not be able to fix everything, but I can snuggle, and that's the next best thing. That's still true more than ten years later.

# 2 | LIVING BEYOND THE BINARY

Our society is rooted in the idea that gender is binary. The most common questions we ask expectant parents are "Do you know what you're having?" and "Boy or girl?" We're obsessed with it. When we check that "girl" or "boy" box, we believe, whether consciously or unconsciously, that it tells us something about that child and who they will be. What toys will they want, and what clothes will they wear? What activities will they enjoy? Who will they marry? What will they do for a living? Many of us say our children can be whoever they're going to be and love whomever they're going to love, but the way we talk and the things we buy say otherwise. This hyper-gendered society is the water in which we've been swimming our entire lives. It's in everything—the books we read, the media we consume, and the stores where we shop. It has settled deep into our knowing in ways that will take generations to unlearn.

Some things are changing, yes. We tell girls they can be anything they want to be. We celebrate women in STEM, politics, athletics, and corporate leadership. As a child, I could not have imagined the kind of representation we're seeing today for women. We have more women in Congress than ever before, and for the first time, the vice president of the United States is a woman. The US National Women's Soccer Team fought and won for equal pay across men and women's soccer, including a settlement of twenty-four million dollars to offset years of inequity. However, boys aren't offered the same celebration when they step outside longstanding expectations of masculinity. Misogyny runs deep as we celebrate girls who embrace more traditionally masculine roles but feel uncomfortable when boys prefer ballet over basketball.

Media representation and celebration of those breaking down gender roles and expectations are growing in powerful and necessary ways, but we still live in a world of elaborate gender reveals and pink and blue toy aisles. Parents who claim they'd love and accept their child if they were LGBTQ+ are raising their children with the assumption they're not LGBTQ+. What does this look like? It looks like jokes about little boys and their future wives. It looks like nurseries decorated with dinosaurs for boys and fairies for girls. It looks like raising a child as if you know who they are before they have a chance to tell you. It looks like failing to create space where they can freely show you who they are without carrying the weight of your expectations.

## PATTERNS, NOT RULES

When I was pregnant with my first child in 2006, I was everything you'd expect from a first-time parent. Filled with equal parts excitement and anxiety, I had no idea what was to come. How can you? Nevertheless, I felt that urge to plan and organize, to nest if you will, creating order and predictability amid so much unknown.

For me, much of that order and predictability hinged on knowing the sex of my baby. I knew there was a lot I couldn't plan for about what was to come, about who this small human growing in my belly would be, but modern medicine told me I could know their sex. Our society told me that was the same as their gender. So I anxiously awaited the moment we'd have the big ultrasound. I'd had an ultrasound earlier in the pregnancy, but all the pregnancy books and the pregnant mommy group I'd found online told me the anatomy scan was usually around twenty weeks. According to them, that was when I'd be able to find out my baby's sex. At the next appointment, I eagerly asked my doctor when we'd get to see what we were having. He looked surprised and said, "They didn't tell you?" My heart sank. He went on to say I must have gone too early to find out the sex, but the ultrasound technician had gotten all the measurements and information they needed. There was no need for another scan. "Well, I guess it'll be a surprise," the doctor said with a shrug.

God bless my partner for enduring the full-on pregnant lady meltdown that ensued. A surprise? No. It could not be a surprise. There were enough surprises in this whole first-time parent pregnancy thing, and I could not handle one more. I was beside myself. How would I know how to decorate the nursery? All the baby's clothes would be yellow and green! My child could not start their life out in this kind of ambiguity.

I hope that at this point, if you were carrying any idea that I had this all right all along, that somehow my raising of a transgender child was without massive missteps and growth, you are now assured otherwise. When I look back on that moment, knowing about our parenting journey and the book you're reading now, I'm reminded how much capacity we each have for learning and growth. Grace abounds. We're all learning. We may start at different places on the journey, but there is no magical finish line where we have it all figured out. We just keep learning.

Back to pregnant Jamie in 2006. My spouse and I did what any reasonable parents-to-be would do. We drove over an hour to a boutique ultrasound place with some cutesy name I can't remember and paid for a simple two-dimensional ultrasound so they could tell us the news we'd been desperately awaiting. We were having a baby boy. Of course, the answer wasn't that simple.

That was my experience in 2006, before gender-reveal parties became a cultural phenomenon. The pressure to gender your child before they're born has significantly increased since then. Parties with elaborate stunts to announce a child's genitalia have become somewhat commonplace, leaving their mark in more ways than one. Gender reveals have been cited as the cause of forest fires, explosions, a plane crash, and multiple deaths.[1] They would be more aptly called *genitalia reveals*, as we don't know a baby's gender until they tell us (but we'll talk about that later). Jenna Karvunidis, widely recognized as the person who started the trend in 2008 when a blog she wrote about her gender-reveal party went viral, has spoken out against the practice not only because of the absurdity and danger involved in some gender-reveal stunts but because Karvunidis's understanding of gender has evolved.[2] The baby at the center of that very first gender reveal is a girl who proudly breaks down gender boxes and continues to teach her mom what it means to be human.

And that's exactly it. While the actual damages to planet, property, and person by these parties is alarming, the idea that we are holding so tightly to assumptions about unborn babies rooted in the dichotomies of penis or vulva, boy or girl, blue or pink does at least as much harm. When I've witnessed gender-reveal moments, the thing that has stuck with me most is the deep emotion people feel in connection to the news. Excited family members watch, phones and cameras ready to capture the special occasion, as the parents-to-be cut the cake, open the balloons, or do whatever else they're going to do. Blue means boy! Pink means girl! I've watched people jump for joy and hug each other in delight. I want to tell them to stop filming, throw out the evidence. May that child never know how excited you all were to find out they supposedly belonged in this binary box. May that child never know the things you decided in that moment were possible or not possible for them because of that news.

I can't emphasize enough that I know good and loving people have gender-reveal parties. Good and loving people who believe they will love and celebrate their child for whoever they may be. They simply don't realize the expectations they're putting on that child's future. I'm not saying you can't dress your little girl in pink or decorate your little boy's room with fire trucks. I'm just suggesting we loosen our grip on our assumptions of what the future will hold. To do that, we must intentionally change our behavior because those assumptions are embedded in us and the world around us. We need to name things out loud. When people talk about all the sports your little boy will play, it means saying, "Or maybe he'll like ballet." When people talk about the sweet dresses your daughter will wear, it means saying, "Or maybe she'll wear a suit." Slowly, over time, with these adjustments, we can hold more loosely to the things we think we know about our children and what it means for their future. When we hold those ideas loosely, it means our children have more freedom to tell us who they are, and it's easier for us to adjust to that information, to that potentially new direction.

Gender Spectrum, a national organization dedicated to supporting families and equipping professionals to create gender-inclusive spaces, talks about this in a way that I find particularly accessible. They distinguish *patterns* from *rules*. Just because many boys don't wear dresses, it doesn't mean boys can't wear dresses. Just because many girls do wear dresses, it doesn't mean that all girls wear dresses. It also allows us to say that it is totally okay to like, do, or wear things that are common for people of your gender, but it's also okay to like, do, or wear things that are not common for people of your gender. While these patterns of behavior exist in our various cultures, they don't have to limit our expression or experience of our gender. While Gender Spectrum uses this idea as a tool for educators and students, I think it's helpful for all of us as human beings to embrace.

## BOY OR GIRL

"Is your kid a boy or a girl?" The little blond girl asked the question like it was no big deal. Each week, my kids and I met up with families in the area to hike and play in the woods. We called it Forest School, but there was a significant emphasis on the forest over school. Some of us were regulars, there every week, while other families popped in or out as their schedule or location allowed. I'd never met this little one before she appeared by my car door. "Hey, is that your kid?" she asked, pointing at my oldest splashing in a puddle nearby. I nodded. She tried again: "Are they a boy or a girl?"

I looked at my child dressed in rainbow polka dots and then back at the little girl expectantly waiting. My voice caught in my throat as I stuttered, "Uh . . . um . . . well, you're going to have to go ask them." I leaned on the car to steady myself, my face flush, as my toddler whined to be unbuckled. Unfazed, the little girl shrugged her shoulders and ran off to play. I felt lightheaded. What kind of parent doesn't know if their kid is a boy or a girl? What is wrong with me? What is wrong with us?

I expect most parents of gender-diverse children have a moment like this or likely many such moments. Our society doesn't prepare parents to raise gender-diverse and transgender children. In fact, while most new parents would admit they don't know much about raising their new baby, they probably assume their child's gender is one thing they do know. In reality, a common question like "Is my child a boy or a girl?" is not simple for many parents. Gender-diverse children defy categorization. They won't fit in this box or that box. Our world isn't built for them.

As Rebekah became increasingly gender-nonconforming, we got this question a lot. People wanted us to categorize her. Where did she fit? At the same time, she began to get increasingly distressed when things were divided by gender. Everything from dance-class attire to goodie bags at birthday parties caused anxiety. People were constantly telling her she needed to pick where she belonged. Boys go there; girls go here. Boys do this; girls do that. It caused an immense amount of stress. She began to avoid any activity where she anticipated there would be some sort of separation by gender.

Support but not encourage—that's what the books and the experts say. Support your child in expressing their gender however feels good and right to them but don't encourage them in any particular direction. It means living in a sort of liminal space for some time. You're not sure if this is a stop on the journey or a final destination, and you won't know until they eventually tell you. So we hold things loosely. We ground ourselves in what we know to be unshakably and undeniably true. They are our children, and we are called to love them unconditionally. They will always be loved and held by the God who created them, and so will we. With those truths as our foundation, we can figure the rest out. We can gift our children time, patience, and attention. We can watch as they come to understand their gender and then as they find ways to articulate that understanding to us.

## CREATING SPACE

During that period of waiting, my spouse and I spent our time reading all the books we could find and connecting to as many support groups as possible. Sometimes we felt like we had a notion of where this journey was taking us, but I don't think either of us could bring ourselves to say it aloud. And more importantly, Rebekah hadn't told us yet. She hadn't said, "Mom and Dad, I'm a girl." It wasn't our job to say it. It was our job to offer her space to get there on her own. So we waited and wondered. We supported. We continued to create space for her to be herself outside of these gendered boxes and advocated for her where we could.

Imagination and pretend play can be a vessel for this exploration. So many transgender teens and adults I know recall vivid years of playing dress-up and losing themselves inside expansive make-believe worlds. Others think back to a special Halloween costume, a time when they were allowed to shake off the rules of their typical everyday existence and try on a different identity. The Halloween before Rebekah transitioned was the very first time she wore a dress in public. She was a fairy princess. She loved that costume so much. She carefully picked each piece—a hand-me-down Easter dress from a friend, turquoise leggings, rainbow fairy wings, a flower crown, and a wand for good measure—and she tried it on many times before the day finally arrived. She was equally excited and anxious. I imagine it felt like a big step for her to go out into the world in that fairy princess dress, an affirming step toward who she was realizing she was. Halloween gave her the space to do that the same way our dress-up bin had been her haven for exploration since she was a toddler.

Beyond pretend spaces, we worked to create space for her to continue exploring what felt truest for her in spaces in her regular life by pushing back on gendered dress codes, gendered activities, and gendered expectations. We did that for years in small ways that accumulated over time. It meant when they had Fun Friday at school, and the boys played with Lego and the girls got little makeovers, we encouraged them to make clear the separation was based on *activity* opposed to *gender*. (Okay, yes, I know how problematic the activity breakdown alone sounds. Fun Friday meant the students got to choose what they did, and this is how things went down. Some of that may have been because of the way children are conditioned by society, but it also may have just been a result of those patterns we talked about. It's okay to behave in ways that align with society's expectations for our gender. We don't free anyone by shaming them for their interests, whatever those may be.)

Differentiating based on activity instead of gender freed Rebekah and the other students to go where they wanted, whether it lined up with gender patterns or not. Generally, when we make things more gender inclusive, it benefits all students, not just gender-expansive students. That is something I'm going to say and show you repeatedly. Being gender inclusive benefits us all. Transgender, nonbinary, or even LGBTQ+ people are not the only ones who need to be freed from the limitations of the binary. We all need it. None of us truly fits into these tiny boxes. We deserve to live in the fullness of our identity. We were each made in God's image, and that image isn't meant to be restricted or kept small.

There were many situations like Fun Friday where we just asked for a little wiggle room for Rebekah to be herself. We advocated for her to choose her clothing for dance class. She didn't want to wear tights and a leotard like the other girls, but she was bored with the white T-shirt and black pants required for boys. The girls got to wear all the colors and designs! So we talked with folks and arranged for Rebekah to wear the black pants she was happy wearing with a shirt in whatever color she liked.

Each time we were able to loosen the rigid gender expectations, we created space for Rebekah to step more fully into herself. She had more permission, more support, and more places where she wasn't being shoved in a box. That space allowed her to start to talk more about her identity. "Maybe I'm a girl?" "I'm not sure I'm a boy who likes pink?" We began seeing a gender therapist, who assured us we were doing the right thing by following our child's lead. The therapist suggested we check in with her each day and let her tell us if she was feeling like a boy or a girl or neither on any given day. Thereafter, we waited each day to find out what Rebekah might share and what we might learn as a result. Looking back, it's all pretty obvious. She never, ever said she was a boy. She'd either say, "I'm a girl" or "I'm not sure." But again, the act of asking the question created more space for Rebekah to step more firmly and fully into herself. It allowed her to test the waters. Each time she said, "I'm a girl" and things didn't come crashing down around her, she grew a little more confident.

At some point when we were firmly living in the in-between, my sister-in-law got engaged and asked four of her youngest nephews, Rebekah included, to be ring bearers at the wedding. (We can talk about the fact that my dear sister-in-law planned on having four ring bearers another day; she's a go-big-or-go-home kind of person. We love her for it.) Rebekah wanted nothing to do with the wedding. Nothing at all. I thought it might be because of the clothing plans they were making (white Converse, navy pants, white button downs, and burgundy suspenders— adorable!). I talked with my sister-in-law, who immediately said, "Of course! She can wear whatever she wants. We'll bedazzle the heck out of her suspenders. We'll add all the bling. We'll make sure she loves it." First, this response was beautiful, and I'm grateful for family who has supported Rebekah in being herself, whatever that looked like, from day one. But somehow, none of that helped Rebekah feel better. She resisted every part of that wedding until she transitioned a few months later and realized she'd get to be the flower girl.

That's the thing about all these gendered roles and spaces. They can be exclusive and suffocating to those who do not fit in the binary, whether that's because, like Rebekah, they are trying to figure out where they fit or because *who* they are doesn't fit inside either box. At the same time, those gendered roles and spaces can be absolutely euphoric when someone feels they are finally where they always should have been. It can be both/and. In more places than not, breaking down the rigid gender expectations and separations is an act of liberation for people of all genders. And being in spaces where you are affirmed and celebrated by people with whom you share common identities, including gender, can be a life-giving and positive experience.

For Rebekah, her gender does fit within the binary. She's a girl. She always has been; we just didn't know. But she also benefits from the ongoing deconstruction of gender expectations that are largely rooted in misogyny and patriarchy. We used to say she could be any kind of boy she wanted to be. Now she can be any kind of girl she wants to be. For others who don't fit in the binary, their gender may be more fluid or expansive. They want the freedom to be any kind of human they want to be. For some young people, a nonbinary identity is a step on the way to a binary one, but for many, they are the truest versions of themselves when not constrained by the labels *boy* or *girl*. They may understand themselves to be a combination of genders, between genders, or something else altogether. For some of us who are new to this, who aren't a part of this generation that embraces people so freely and fully, it can make your head spin.

Adults can easily be overwhelmed with the concept of gender diversity, and we'll address that in the next chapter. But first, we can learn from the young people in our lives how simple this can be. The little girl at Forest School who asked if Rebekah was a boy or a girl ran off to talk to Rebekah. Rebekah doesn't remember how she answered the question or even if the little girl asked it, but moments after they met, the two were skipping through the woods. As kids do, they went off holding hands, accepting each other for exactly who they were at that moment. I want to be just like them when I grow up.

# 3 | WORDS MATTER

The day Rebekah learned the word *transgender*, something clicked inside her. Outwardly, she appeared to be an eight-year-old boy dressed head to toe in pink, but after years of gender-nonconforming behavior, she had started to say things like "I'm not really a boy" and "I think I'm a girl." She was cautiously exploring what that meant. As much as she didn't fit into gender boxes neatly, Rebekah was absolutely a check-all-the-boxes kind of kid. She liked rules and organization, and she thrived in structured settings. She wanted to meet the expectations of those around her, and it was especially hard for her to reconcile her identity being such a radical departure from what the world wanted from her.

Preparing to go swimming at her younger brother's birthday party in February, she realized she had no idea what to wear. Her wardrobe had shifted since the summer. She now exclusively wore clothes from the girls' section of stores, but she hadn't considered bathing suits. That day, she'd wear what was in her closet, but it started a larger conversation. I gave her all the options for the coming summer. We could try to find pink swim trunks. We could get a pink rash guard. My chest tightened as I offered, "Or you could wear a girl's bathing suit." I knew that would be complicated at best, but we would just have to figure it out if that's what she wanted.

At a loss for any other options, I sat with her, and we googled "gender-nonconforming swimsuits." There weren't many results that day, but I am glad to say there are more if you perform that same search all these years later. One of the search results was a website that had the acronym LGBT on it. "Do you know what those letters mean?" I asked. She didn't. We were a family that had always taught our children that love is love. I remember us squealing with delight as a family in the backyard when we got the news of the Supreme Court decision on marriage equality, but we'd never talked about the acronym LGBT. I went through the letters one at a time. When I got to the T and explained what it means to be transgender, her face lit up. "Oh, maybe that's what I am." Oh. Maybe that's what you are. Deep breaths.

From that moment to the day she went out into the world for the first time as herself, as Rebekah, it was just six weeks. Six weeks of learning even more, seeking community, talking with a gender therapist, and consulting with our family doctor. For Rebekah, having language that described what she'd been feeling inside for so long and knowing there was a community that came with that language changed everything.

Acknowledging and understanding the language and termi-nology is important, and we're about to get into all of it. But first, please know there's not going to be a quiz. You don't have to memorize all of this. In fact, you don't need to know all the words or terminology to show up in love and support for trans-gender and gender-diverse children. That's an especially good thing because language for gender and identity is constantly evolving. Even if we do become well versed in these terms, we should prepare for the meanings of words to change over time and for the introduction of new words too. In fact, after this book is published, the terminology presented here may become out-dated. The contents of this book reflect the current language and understanding to the best of my ability, and if you're reading this after terminology has shifted and understanding has evolved, I ask for your grace. Know that I plan to evolve and shift too, but the words in these pages will stay put.

Instead of focusing on memorizing all the words and definitions and getting stuck on the things you don't understand, be present with the person in front of you. As a cisgender person, I will never fully understand what it means to be transgender or nonbinary, and that's okay. People with dominant identities sometimes feel like something isn't valid unless they can understand it. But we can trust people when they tell us who they are, and we can listen to the language they use to describe themselves and mirror that language back to them. Above all else, even if we don't understand all the letters in an acronym or what it means to be nonbinary, for example, we have to know that those words and identities are legitimate and worthy of honor and respect.

The terminology around transgender, nonbinary, and gender-diverse identities can be overwhelming. Wrapping our brain around what it means to be transgender is not easy for people who have never really had to think about their gender. However, the language is important. To support and affirm the gender-diverse and transgender children in our lives, we need to have a foundation of shared understanding. So let's break down the basics of sex, gender identity, gender expression, and sexual orientation. While this book has nothing to do with sexual orientation, it is all too often confused with gender identity and expression, so we will cover them all.

## SEX

First, we look at sex. The sex assigned at birth is the body piece of the puzzle. When babies are born (or often beforehand, as I covered in the ultrasound debacle of 2006), we declare, "It's a boy!" or "It's a girl!" This is based on the external genitalia we see. We might as well be saying, "That's a penis!" or "There's a vulva!" We are generally taught that the question of sex is simply a check-this-box-or-that box situation. In reality, sex assigned at birth is not limited to the binary. People with intersex traits have variations in genitalia, chromosomes, hormones, or reproductive organs. Sometimes, intersex traits are known at birth; other times, intersex traits may be discovered at puberty or later in life.

It used to be standard practice for many children born with intersex traits to undergo surgery at a young age to assimilate their genitalia and reproductive organs, aligning them with typically developing genitalia and reproductive organs. Doctors and parents likely advocated for these procedures to protect a child from being othered or being aware of their differences, but these procedures are increasingly understood to be a violation of bodily autonomy. In some circumstances, surgery may be medically necessary, but interventions that are not medically necessary cause more harm than any potential or perceived benefits—physically and emotionally. Amnesty International describes these unnecessary procedures as a human rights violation,[1] and organizations like interAct: Advocates for Intersex Youth advocate for the evolution of policy and the protection of children born with intersex traits.

While people may assume intersex traits are rare, it is estimated that 1.7 percent of the population have at least one intersex trait, and 0.5 percent meet the clinical criteria for an intersex condition. Some say the incidence of people with intersex traits is comparable to the number of people with red hair in the world. It's a tangible way for people to understand that intersex traits are not as rare as they may have thought. Red hair or no red hair, it is a fact that people with intersex traits exist. They exist, and they are a part of God's good creation. And biological sex may not be as simple, or as binary, as most of us once believed.

## GENDER IDENTITY

Next, we have gender identity. Gender identity is who you know yourself to be. It is a deeply held sense of self. *Gender* and *gender identity* can be used interchangeably. We cannot know someone's gender identity unless they tell us, but we make assumptions about people's gender identity all the time. Those assumptions are usually based on their gender expression, but we'll get to that in a minute.

People whose gender identity aligns with the sex they were assigned at birth are cisgender. That's me. When I was born, the people around me said, "It's a girl," and I deeply know myself to be a girl. People whose gender identity does not align with the sex they were assigned at birth are transgender. That's my daughter. When she was born, everyone said, "It's a boy," but she deeply knows herself to be a girl. *Transgender* and *cisgender* are both adjectives. That means we use them to describe someone. We can talk about transgender girls, transgender boys, or transgender people. We don't use it as a noun ("those transgenders"), and it's never a verb. It's not appropriate to add the *-ed* suffix. People do not transgender into another gender. There is no transgender fairy who shows up to bop them on the head with their magic gender wand and transgender them. It'd be like saying someone is "gayed." It's not something that happens to you; it's a word that describes part of who you are. *Transgender* and *cisgender* are sometimes shortened to *trans* and *cis* for shorthand.

Gender identity is not simply a matter of being either a man or a woman. We sometimes think of it as a continuum or a spectrum with man on one end and woman on the other, and in between we have identities like nonbinary, agender, gender fluid, genderqueer, and more. Or perhaps we imagine nonbinary identities as something like a twist ice cream cone, with chocolate and vanilla spiraled together. Some nonbinary people may feel exactly like that, but for others, it may instead be a different flavor altogether or perhaps no flavor at all. People who don't identify exclusively as a man or a woman may feel like they are a mix of genders, may understand themselves to exist outside of gender, or their understanding of their gender may not be entirely fixed but more malleable.

This is where I remind you that you don't have to know or understand all the words people use to describe themselves. I've been doing this work for years, and I am still learning new words and language. Words and the way we use them change over time, and younger generations, in particular, are always finding new ways to describe their innermost self to those of us on the outside. It's beautiful, actually. I think that's a helpful perspective shift. We can be frustrated by there always being new things to learn, or we can look at the beauty of seeing new aspects of a person's identity being articulated with language for the first time, the same way we might marvel at works of art that show us something we'd never considered or imagined. I choose to see the beauty.

When we start to feel overwhelmed by the language and terminology, our first instinct can be to get defensive. *How am I supposed to know all these words? I don't have time for this. Why are they making this so complicated? I don't need all these labels; I just see people as human beings.* Instead, what if when we were confronted with something new we didn't understand, we paused? We took a deep breath. Then we shifted the narrative. It could sound something like this:

> *Here is what I know to be true. I don't know all these words or meanings, but these words are important to someone I care about. Not only are they important to someone I care about, but that someone is trying to share them with me. What a gift! Someone I care about is trying to find language to describe who they are in the most authentic sense and share that with me and other people who care about them. That is brave, beautiful, and blessing-filled work. So even if I feel like I can't quite keep up, I can listen intently to what the people in my life are telling me, and I can know that these words are deeply important to them even if I don't fully understand the terminology.*

## GENDER EXPRESSION

Next, we have gender expression. As the name would suggest, gender expression is how we express our gender to the people around us. This is the social part of our gender. It's how we walk, talk, move our bodies, dress, wear our hair, and more. Sometimes we also think of this on a continuum from male to female with androgynous in the middle. We make assumptions about people's gender identity based on our perception of their gender expression, but they are just that—assumptions. Gender expression is separate from but not unrelated to gender identity. Gender expression can also change day to day or month to month. For me, for instance, there are days when I may present in a more androgynous way with a baseball hat, jeans, sneakers, and hooded sweatshirt. Other days, I may choose to dress up for a special occasion in a more feminine way, wearing a dress and high heels with makeup and jewelry. (That's admittedly pretty rare for me.) Regardless of how I dress, my gender identity doesn't change.

I think many people who don't identify in the LGBTQ+ community assume that they exist on the ends of these continuum, that their identities and expressions are those binary boxes that anchor the spectrum. Even people who have come to understand the complexity and nuance in gender may still default to the idea that our society's binary understanding of gender is the norm. They just admit there are people who exist outside of that norm. We're going to come back to that idea of the norm, but first let's step back and think more carefully about where we each exist on the continuum.

When I teach this content in workshops, I usually ask participants to tell me the most feminine public figure they can think of. Answers vary based on the demographic of the group (including age, race, ethnicity, and culture) but usually include people like Beyoncé, Kim Kardashian, Marilyn Monroe, Pamela Anderson, or even fictional characters like Cinderella. That's quite a group, and it communicates a lot about what we believe about femininity. I am a cisgender woman who can express my gender in feminine ways, but I don't *ever* express my gender in a way that looks like any of those people. So if I think about a continuum of masculine to feminine, I'm never going to place myself on the extreme end of that. I generally live a bit more toward the middle.

We can do the same thing when we think about masculine presentations. When I ask workshop participants about the most masculine public figures they can recall, overwhelmingly I get Dwayne "The Rock" Johnson, Arnold Schwarzenegger, or, if we're going the Disney route, Hercules or Gaston. I am married to a wonderful man, a man who was assigned male at birth and who expresses his gender in a typically masculine way, and his gender expression looks nothing like Dwayne "The Rock" Johnson. (I write this with his full agreement.) Even though his sex, gender, and expression fit mostly into society's expectations, his gender expression doesn't actually lie on the far end of the continuum. That doesn't make his gender identity any less valid. He is still just as much a man as someone who expresses their gender in a more hypermasculine way. He knows himself to be a man, and he's a man regardless of his gender expression on any given day. There is much more room for nuance and diversity of expression when we don't try to force ourselves into that box or this box.

Of course, those boxes and this continuum are all deeply rooted in society's expectations and beliefs about femininity and masculinity. What we consider to be masculine and feminine is anchored to this particular space and this particular time. For instance, if we look back at white American society in the early 1900s, the color pink was not the symbol of femininity that it has come to be. It was considered stronger and more suitable for boys.[2] Similarly, our understanding of femininity has expanded over the years (if only slightly) to include things like wearing pants and working outside the home. If we travel around the world and look at different cultures, we'll see that understandings of femininity and masculinity change as well. In Scotland, men wear kilts, something that fits the modern definition of a skirt. That's not considered typical here in the United States. Even in the twenty-first-century United States, our rich cultural diversity means there are a multitude of ideas of gender intersecting with the dominant white culture.

The term *gender nonconforming* refers to people who don't conform to society's standards of what it means to be a man or a woman as defined by that place and time. Their gender expression doesn't fit in the box that came with their sex assigned at birth and/or their gender identity. This could be based on their physical appearance—how they dress, wear their hair, talk, walk, and move through the world. Or it could be based on their behavior or roles—how they navigate relationships, family life, or the workplace. Sometimes it's both. Someone who is gender nonconforming may be a part of the LGBTQ+ community or not. They may always present in gender-nonconforming ways, or they may express themselves sometimes in gender-nonconforming ways. For folks whose gender nonconformity is deeply connected to who they are, words like *gender expansive*, *gender creative*, or *gender diverse* may feel right for them.

Gender expression is messy. It's wrapped up in cultural and societal understandings and expectations around gender, and it is impacted by perception. While gender identity is exclusively determined by the individual, gender expression is something experienced in relation to others. It is publicly considered, debated, and judged. Sometimes we may understand ourselves to be expressing our gender in one way while it's received or perceived in a different way altogether. Many people must consider their safety as a factor in their gender expression. This may mean someone expresses their gender in a way that does not feel the most authentic or congruent with who they know themselves to be in order to be safer as they move about the world. There is beauty, complexity, nuance, and vulnerability in the mess of who we know ourselves to be, how we are able to express ourselves to the world, and how we understand ourselves in relation to each other.

## SEXUAL ORIENTATION

Let's jump to the last piece of identity we're going to look at: sexual orientation. Sexual orientation, sometimes referred to as sexual identity, describes to whom we experience attraction. It is entirely separate from the three other facets of our identities (sex, gender identity, gender expression) I've described thus far. When I was explaining to the world that my eight-year-old daughter was transgender, the first question was overwhelmingly "What does an eight-year-old know about sexuality?" To be honest, she didn't know a lot about sexuality then, although it's worth noting that as a part of normal and appropriate development, children begin to understand their sexuality far earlier than most people assume. However, my daughter didn't need to know her sexual identity to know her gender identity. Gender identity is about who you are, whereas sexual orientation is about to whom you experience romantic or sexual attraction. Sexual orientation can also be described as a continuum, with attraction to women on one end and attraction to men on the other. In the middle, there are identities like asexual, bisexual, pansexual, and polysexual.

Once again, you do not need to know what all the words mean to understand that they are legitimate identities and matter deeply to the people who use them to describe themselves. Just like we make assumptions about people's gender identity based on their gender expression, we make assumptions about people's sexual orientation based on their past or present relationships. This results in a significant amount of erasure of the identities that don't exist on the ends of the continuum. Bisexual and pansexual people are attracted to people of more than one gender, and so when we put them into a box based on a single relationship, we are erasing part of who they are.

A common misconception about people who experience attraction to people of more than one gender is that it must mean they always act on that attraction. This misconception suggests that bisexual, pansexual, and polysexual people are, by definition, non-monogamous. That's simply not true. People who are monogamous, including straight people and gay people, may experience attraction to someone who isn't their committed partner. They simply don't act on that attraction because of the mutually agreed upon understanding of their relationship expectations and parameters. People who are attracted to people of more than one gender are no more likely to be non-monogamous than people who are only attracted to people of one gender. And we can only know someone's sexual orientation if they tell us.

Do you see a theme here? We can't know people unless we listen to who they tell us they are. Most importantly, we respect self-identification. That means I'm going to trust that you know yourself better than I could ever know you, and I'm going to expect that you trust that I know myself better than you could ever know me. We have to extend that trust to all the people in our lives, including our children. As parents, especially, this can be hard. We have such intimate knowledge of these small humans in our lives, but the truth is they know themselves better than even we can know them. That doesn't make us bad parents. Their understanding and articulation of who they are will grow, expand, and even shift as they get older, but it is a powerful act of trust, value, and love to believe people when they tell us who they are.

## BEYOND THE CONTINUUM

Now that we have a basic understanding of sex, gender identity, gender expression, and sexual orientation, and we understand that there is a rainbow of possibility in each of these elements—a continuum rather than a simple binary—we have to throw out the concept of the continuum. Yep, you heard that right. I'm sorry, but it's the next step of our evolution.

The continuum suggests there are norms. That's why those of us who are a part of the dominant culture are inclined to situate ourselves on the ends of each continuum, in those places we understand to be typical. The end points of each spectrum or continuum tell us what is considered normal or typical in each of these facets of our identity—sex, gender, gender expression, and sexual orientation. The end points communicate that these are the points around which we should orient ourselves—male or female, man or woman, masculine or feminine, attracted to women or men. These binary categories anchor us in what is "normal."

The idea of a continuum is helpful in that it creates space for us to admit that so much more exists outside of those binary boxes; however, when we continue to define ourselves in relation to society's assumed norms, we chain ourselves to them. We limit ourselves to only knowing who we are in relation to the boxes in which we do not fit. In reality, people who hold identities that don't fall at the ends of our continuum don't feel like they exist halfway between this norm or that norm. Many people with a nonbinary gender identity may not feel that "in between man and woman" quite fits their experience. Remember the ice cream cone. Sure, there are twist cones, with chocolate and vanilla swirled together, but there are also entirely other flavors to consider.

Instead of a linear continuum, we might consider that each of these pieces of identity fit more into a rainbow gradient sphere, where there are no ends or points. Jeffrey Marsh, an author and educator, describes gender as a blob instead of a continuum. It's much more fluid and flexible than what most of us understand. I find it helpful to teach these concepts with a continuum first because of the world we live in and the background most of us who are new to these conversations bring. It's hard to jump from where we are to where we eventually want to be in terms of understanding. Instead, we can create steps along the way to evolve our understanding. So we learn one thing, and then we throw it out to embrace something truer. As my daughter often says, we are not trying to create more boxes for people to fit in. We are trying to break them down so that all people can show up more fully and freely as their truest selves because the world is a more beautiful, more colorful, and healthier place when we do.

## PRONOUNS

Beyond words that specifically describes our identities like *transgender* and *nonbinary*, we use language every day that is gendered.

We do it without even thinking. Pronouns are perhaps the most basic gendered piece of language. It's fascinating how a simple, innocuous part of language has become such a lightning-rod topic. Pronouns are words that we use to refer to a person in place of their name. I tried three times to write that sentence without using a pronoun (their), and I couldn't do it. Pronouns are important because they communicate gender. Men and boys in our culture usually use pronouns like *he*, *him*, and *his*. *The boy waved goodbye to his friends.* Women and girls often use *she*, *her*, and *hers*. *The woman took her dog for a walk.* That seems pretty simple until we remember that while we assume people's gender based on gender expression, we can't actually know their gender unless they tell us.

We attribute pronouns to people based on our assumptions. Most of the time, we're right, but other times we get it wrong. It doesn't feel good when people around us wrongly assume things about us. It leaves us feeling unseen and unknown. If you've never had the experience of someone using pronouns that don't fit you, you may never have had to think about this. That's a privilege that comes with fitting into the dominant culture's expectations of gender. As someone assigned female at birth, who identifies as a woman, and fits mostly into the gender expectations our society has for women, I've never had someone meet me and use *he* or *him*. At the same time, like I mentioned earlier, because I have a name that is often used for boys and girls, I do find that customer service representatives or people reaching out to me in writing, whether email or postal mail, occasionally assume I'm a man. I'm always a little taken aback. It generally doesn't feel good. Sharing pronouns has become an important practice in creating more inclusive spaces. You may see people's pronouns in their email signatures, on their social media bios, or on their name tags at events. Perhaps you've met someone who has shared their pronouns with you.

In addition to male and female gendered pronouns, pronouns like *they* and *them* can be used to refer to multiple people or to describe a single person whose gender doesn't fit into the binary of boy or girl. Contrary to the belief of many, this is not new, and it is grammatically correct. The *Oxford English Dictionary* traces singular *they* back to the year 1375, where it appears in the medieval romance *William and the Werewolf*.[3] Of perhaps greater relevance, we use the singular *they* regularly when referring to someone whose gender is unknown. If I walked into an empty room and found a cell phone sitting on the desk, I might say, "Oh! Someone left their phone here. I hope they come back and get it. Not having it must be stressful for them."

It does take practice to shift the way we use language, whether that's changing the pronouns we use to refer to someone we've known for a long time or just getting used to using singular *they* in regular conversation. That's okay. It's okay to need some time to adjust, and you're likely going to make mistakes. And we must put in the work. Practice, practice, practice. When you mess up, correct yourself quickly and move on. Avoid making it a big thing or making it all about you. This happens when we say things like "Oh my gosh, I am trying, but this is just so hard." If you don't even realize you've made a mistake and a person corrects you, say thank you and move on. When we are dramatic with our apology, telling the person how hard we're working, it puts the person we just harmed, albeit unintentionally, in a position to be obligated to make us feel better. That doesn't serve them. It serves you. Take a breath. Say thank you. Keep trying.

Sometimes when we're in that practicing phase, it can be good to avoid pronouns altogether and use their name as much as possible instead.

Some people use multiple pronouns. They may use *she/they* or *he/they*. What that means may be a little different for each person. It may be that in some settings they prefer one pronoun over the other. Or it may be that both feel great to them, and they invite people to use them interchangeably. As we, as a society, continue to unpack the restrictions that various cultural ideas of gender have put on us, I expect more and more people will find new language to describe themselves or to free themselves to show up as their most real selves. Beyond the pronouns we've discussed, some people also use what are called neopronouns. Some examples include xe/xem/xyr, ze/hir/hirs, and ey/em/eir.

## WHAT DO ALL THOSE LETTERS MEAN?

One final thing: acronyms. So often people get overwhelmed by all the letters. Remember, you do not need to memorize everything to love and support people, and still we need to know that those acronyms are important to the people whose identities are reflected in them. Please don't dismiss or diminish them by not even trying to get them right or intentionally adding letters that don't belong to be funny. LGBTQ+ is an acronym for lesbian, gay, bisexual, transgender, queer with a plus to indicate that there are limitless ways to describe our sexual orientations as well as gender identities and expression. Sometimes you may see the acronym LGBTQIA+ used, which includes letters for intersex and asexual/agender. Other variations of the acronym include 2S for two-spirit people, an identity connected to Indigenous communities in America that we'll talk about more in the next chapter. Another acronym you may come across is TGNC or TGNCNB. These stand for transgender and gender nonconforming or transgender, gender nonconforming, and nonbinary. These are used to specify that we're talking about the gender-based identities in the LGBTQ+ community opposed to the wider community. Finally, one more acronym you may see is SOGIE. Unlike the others described here, SOGIE doesn't refer to a part of the community or specific identities; it stands for sexual orientation, gender identity, and (gender) expression. If I were delivering the content in this chapter in a workshop, I might call it SOGIE 101. These are the foundational elements to understanding LGBTQ+ identities.

Deep breath. That was a lot. Take a moment and check in with yourself. How does this information feel in your body? Are you overwhelmed? Are you excited? Can you locate the sensation? Whatever you're feeling is valid. Acknowledge it. Affirm it.

Take another deep breath. Know that whatever you're feeling, you are a beloved child of God learning more about God's creation and how to show up in love for the people around you. That is a beautiful thing.

One more breath. You don't have to understand this all. You don't have to remember all the words. There is no quiz. Listen to the way the people around you describe themselves and mirror that language back to them. Most of all, believe them when they trust you enough to tell you who they are. That's a gift.

# 4 | FAMILIES IN TRANSITION

People wonder why there is a "sudden" prevalence of transgender and gender-diverse people in the world. There is and isn't. We are seeing increasing numbers of people openly identifying as transgender as a result of increasing visibility, support, resources, and acceptance. According to a 2022 Pew Research study,[1] about 1.6 percent of the population identifies as transgender. That same survey showed that approximately 5.1 percent of adults under thirty identify as transgender. We're seeing the same kind of generational increase across the spectrum of LGBTQ+ identities. In fact, a 2021 Gallup poll[2] showed that 7.1 percent of the population identified as part of the LGBTQ+ community, which is double what it was in 2012 when Gallup first collected this data. But even more significant, when we look at Gen Z adults, that number is 21 percent. It's not that there is something in the water, and it's not the GMOs in our food. It's not even that there are more LGBTQ+ people in the world. It's that more people are willing and able to name and claim their identity. As more and more people share their fullest selves, they create space for others to do the same. Through it all, younger generations, who are less burdened by the way things have always been, are leading the way.

Sex and gender diversity is not a new thing. We see evidence of biological sex diversity in animals, insects, and marine life. Gynandromorph butterflies have one wing that has a male pattern and color while the other wing has a female pattern. Gynandromorphism occurs in insects, birds like chickens or cardinals, and crustaceans like crabs and lobsters. Meanwhile, in seahorses, we see a departure from typical sex roles as the female deposits its fertilized eggs into the male to carry them. In 2016, news broke of five female lionesses in Botswana growing manes and participating in more male-centric behavior like increased roaring and more frequently marking territory with their scent.[3] Approximately 40 percent of male marsh harriers develop a permanent female-like appearance.[4]

At the same time, we see human gender diversity in cultures throughout history and around the world. In North America, many Indigenous communities recognize two-spirit people[5] who function in their communities as outside of male and female genders. Some recognize two-spirit as a third gender, while other communities have distinct terms for two-spirit people who were assigned male at birth and those who were assigned female at birth, creating four kinds of genders. Two-spirit is a general term, while each tribe has its own distinct language and understanding of these individuals in its communities. Third-gender people have been revered throughout history, the hijra in Southeast Asia[6] being one of the largest groups. Hijras are assigned male at birth and express their gender in feminine ways. Traditionally, hijras were respected and honored in Hindu culture, but the arrival of British colonists in the nineteenth and twentieth centuries changed that. Today, they are still fighting the stigma and discrimination that colonialism brought. In Albania, burrnesha were assigned female at birth,[7] dressed and lived as men, and took a vow of celibacy based on a tradition dating back five hundred years rooted in patriarchy. Like gender-diverse and third-gender people in so many cultures, burrnesha were not ridiculed but revered. These are just a few examples out of hundreds of cultures that understand or understood gender to be far more expansive than the binary of man and woman.

## TELLING US WHO THEY ARE

Gender is a mix of the cultural and the personal. We are constantly seeking congruence between our bodies, who we know ourselves to be, and what the world understands about us. These pieces of gender—body, identity, and expression—are things we come to understand and articulate over time. Generally, by age two, most children understand the difference between men and women, boys and girls, and by age three, they can articulate their own gender. This can be true for transgender children in the same way it is for cisgender children. While some transgender children don't articulate their gender until later (likely due to being strongly socialized to act in alignment with the sex they were assigned at birth), generally transgender children have similar gender development to their cisgender peers. They know themselves just like their peers do, and when studied, transgender children behave and develop in similar ways to peers of their affirmed gender.[8] To put it another way, studies show that transgender girls behave and develop like cisgender girls, and transgender boys behave and develop like cisgender boys.

Some transgender children may start by telling us who they are with their words, but often, they start by showing us who they are with their gender expression. Other times, they start asking questions about their body, for example, asking when their vulva will turn into a penis or wanting to get rid of their penis. There is not one right or wrong way. There is no singular sign that declares a child to be transgender. Instead, over time, we see that transgender children are consistent, persistent, and insistent in their gender. They may also experience distress around their socialized gender or their body not matching their identity; that distress is called gender dysphoria.

Critics of a gender-affirming approach take issue with children transitioning, claiming that expression is being equated with identity. They believe parents and practitioners are forcing children who express their gender in unconventional ways to transition to a gender that aligns with their behavior. That's simply not the case. As we've talked about in the prior chapters, many children and adults express their gender in ways that are different from their peers of the same gender. It doesn't mean they're transgender. We must remember the idea of patterns, not rules. Most boys don't wear dresses; some boys do. Nothing about that statement suggests that boys who wear dresses are girls. But we also know the "patterns, not rules" practice applies to bodies as well. Most boys have penises; some do not. Most girls have vulvas; some do not. Most children are not transgender, regardless of their gender presentation; some children are transgender.

The criticism is compounded by the ways that many transgender children do begin to show us who they are with their expression. Whenever we share Rebekah's story and she explains how she always gravitated to typically feminine things, people are quick to point out that liking pink doesn't make you a girl, liking sequins and sparkles and dresses doesn't make you a girl. They are correct. Those aren't the things that make Rebekah a girl.

Still, from the time she could talk, consciously or unconsciously, Rebekah used the language, assumptions, and systems around her to communicate where she belonged. Gender *is* cultural. The world was saying, "This is who you are; this is what boys like," and she immediately knew that didn't fit. So with every choice she made, with every box she refused to squeeze into, she was telling us who she is. Dressed head to toe in pink, she was telling us where to categorize her.

I am not a fan of pink, and I'm not a super-feminine girl. I remember laughing with my spouse about having a little boy dressed head to toe in pink when we wouldn't have wanted that for a little girl! Even if we knew she was a girl from the start, we still wouldn't have surrounded her with pink and purple, sequins and sparkles. That wasn't our style, but that's what Rebekah wanted.

Eventually, sometime after she transitioned, after she had settled into who she was, she was finally able to trust that she didn't have to convince everyone around her of her gender every step of the way. That's when she let go of the pink obsession. She was able to loosen her grip on all things stereotypically "girly" in her own time. Now her favorite color is navy blue. Tomorrow, it could be something else. She mountain bikes and plays field hockey. She loves science and math. She plays clarinet and loves musical theater. For years, she almost never wore dresses, and now she sometimes rocks a dress and fancy shoes with higher heels than I can manage. We still say colors and clothes are for everyone, but for Rebekah, it was never about the clothes or the colors. It was about telling the world who she was in a language they would understand.

We saw this play out in the people around her, the people who loved her. The Christmas before she turned eight, before she transitioned, Rebekah asked for a bike. Specifically, she asked for a bike that was pink and purple with rainbows, sparkles, and unicorns. She was explicit and insistent. My dad, her grandpa, was known in our family as the gifter of bikes. He'd bought all the grandkids bikes for Christmas at one point, and when they outgrew them, he was ready to buy the next one. It was just his thing. As I gave him Christmas lists that year, I explained that Rebekah was ready for a new bike. He said, "Okay, what kind?" I told him her exact words—a pink-and-purple bike with rainbows, sparkles, and unicorns. He knew Rebekah loved pink and purple. Every other item on her Christmas list that year followed the color scheme of pink, purple, and sparkly. He hadn't minded any of those. But the bike hit differently. He said, "Well, it needs to be a boy's bike. They're just different." Surprised, I stumbled over my words in reply: "Maybe just try to find anything in those colors." We hung up.

Of course, boys' and girls' bikes are built differently. Boys' bikes have a straight bar that goes from the base of the handlebars to just below the seat. Girls' bikes have a curved piece that dips down instead of going straight across. This stems from a time when girls exclusively wore dresses, and the lower frame allowed them to mount and dismount their bike without flashing their underwear to everyone nearby. That's the reason. But our culture has come to understand that there is one kind of bike for boys and one kind of bike for girls. We assume there must be some good reason for it without considering that there is very little difference physically between an eight-year-old girl and an eight-year-old boy. The need for distinction between the genders and what belongs to each of them is ingrained in us.

My dad called me back a few days later to say he realized it was silly, and he'd get her the bike she'd like best. And he did. On the day we celebrated Christmas with them, she sat with her eyes covered as he wheeled in a pink-and-purple bike with rainbows, sparkles, and My Little Ponies. It may not have had unicorns, but it was darn close. She opened her eyes and squealed in delight. That was the sound of a child teaching the adults in her life what mattered and what didn't. Bikes are like colors and clothes. They're for everyone. And if you have the opportunity to choose sparkles, do it.

## BECAUSE I'M A GIRL

Rebekah began to tell us who she was by the things she liked and the way she dressed, but eventually, she tried out some words. Shortly after her eighth birthday, just a few weeks after the pink-and-purple-bike Christmas, we planned a small birthday celebration at a painting studio for Rebekah and two of her friends. Like most of her friends, they were girls. Her little brother, Elijah, was almost six years old. Her friends also had little brothers. So Elijah and the two other little brothers were going to tag along. I promise all this background matters.

As we were getting ready to leave the house, Rebekah said to Elijah, "There will be three boys and three girls at the painting place today." Elijah did some quick math in his head and looked confused. He may have been only five years old, but he knew this didn't add up. Rebekah saw the question on his face and added,

"Because I'm a girl." Oh. Hmm. This was new. I stopped what I was doing so I could listen more closely, doing my best to stay calm and not draw attention to myself. Like any little sibling, Elijah wasn't about to let her trick him; he knew the math wasn't right. He said, "But you're a boy." Rebekah had been waiting for this moment and calmly declared, "No, I'm a girl."

There it is. She said it. The thing we'd been wondering. She said it aloud. How would Elijah react? I felt like time had stopped. God bless that little boy of mine; Elijah didn't even pause. He didn't gawk or react. He just said, as if it was a perfectly reasonable thing to say, "Oh, you want us to call you a girl?" Rebekah nodded. Elijah shrugged. "Well, you just never told me before, so I didn't know. I will." That was it. It was that simple. I released the breath I hadn't realized I'd been holding. She had said her truth aloud, and her brother had received it with grace. Maybe we could do this. Maybe it was going to be alright.

My mom lived with us at the time. She came downstairs moments later, arms full of laundry to fold. Rebekah clearly felt pretty good based on how the conversation went with her little brother, and she excitedly told her mema, "There are going to be three girls and three boys there today." She paused and then added, "Because I'm a girl." My mom was (and is) a wonderfully supportive grandmother and mother. She watched up close, a part of our household, as Rebekah's gender journey unfurled. She worked hard to keep up with the evolution of Rebekah's likes and dislikes, to adjust to her style choices and evolving gender expression, and to unpack a lifetime of gender expectations. In that moment, my mom, who wildly loves her grandkids and was doing her very best, heard Rebekah's declaration and burst out laughing. Rebekah absorbed her mema's reaction and burst into tears.

When my mom realized what she had done, she was crushed. She hadn't meant to cause harm. She laughed out of confusion, out of fear. No one had prepared her for this. That's where most of us start. No one has prepared us for this. Our children continue to teach us, to teach everyone in their lives, and we do our best to keep up. Luckily, we don't do it alone.

I think often of the disciples when Jesus met them on the Road to Emmaus (Luke 24:13–35). They were deep in their own grief and fear. They didn't recognize Jesus when he joined them, and as they walked together, they told him of all that had gone down. Jesus listened to their despair and their confusion, and then he explained how everything needed to happen the way it did. He taught them. Maybe he was patient; maybe he wasn't. Still, he brought them along on this journey, and later that night when they broke bread together, their eyes were opened. They said, "Were not our hearts burning within us while he was talking to us on the road, while he was opening the scriptures to us?"[9] Then they left for Jerusalem, where they would tell everyone what they had learned.

Jesus steps into our places of grief and confusion and walks with us. Jesus stepped in my mom's place of grief and confusion and walked with her. She prayed and read the books I offered her. She watched the documentaries. She asked her questions. And she listened to her grandchild. When Rebekah eventually transitioned, my mom saw the weight lift off her shoulders. She saw Rebekah light up from the inside out. And my mom's heart burned, and she had to go and tell everyone. She told her friends. She told the ladies from work. She told her eightysomething-year-old parents. She had been so worried about the world, about what people would think, about what this would mean for

Rebekah's future, but with her fears tended to and her heart on fire, she went and told the story of all that had happened. She walked with others in their confusion and fear. She changed hearts and minds. God works through each of us to help others on the journey. And all those people she told? In time, they would take the story to tell others. Time and time again, Jesus steps into our places of grief, walks with us, and leaves our hearts burning and ready to go tell the world the good news.

## GRIEF

One of the questions I am most asked is how it felt for *me* when my child transitioned. Was there grief? Was there pain? How did you handle it? These are human questions, but sometimes the questions feel like they are for the benefit of the person asking, a lurid curiosity. These questions aren't about understanding better how we show up in community together, but they seem instead focused on the drama of it all, as if people are watching the latest series on Netflix. *Please, tell me how hard it was.* At best, these questions are rooted in a narrative that centers the experience of people who love transgender people opposed to transgender people themselves. At worst, they center the curiosity of cisgender people who have never met a transgender person (to their knowledge). It suggests that it's somehow *hard* to love a transgender child. But that's not true. I will never allow the primary narrative around my transgender child finally getting to be herself in the world to be that it was so difficult for me. Watching my child step into herself, watching her joy explode and her light shine brighter than ever before, was a true and deep joy. That being said, it is fair to say there was more to the journey.

The topic of grief can be a lightning rod in support communities for parents of transgender children. Some transgender youth and adults have expressed pain and frustration around the idea that their parents had to grieve them when they were still alive; in fact, they were more alive than ever. At the same time, many parents describe feelings of grief and sadness as a very real part of their journey. I'm going to be so bold as to say that these two things are simultaneously true: feelings of grief, sadness, and fear are normal amid the uncertainty of a child's transition, *and* the pain and frustration we hear from the transgender community around this narrative of grief can teach us how to better care for our kids and articulate our feelings.

We never felt sadness that our daughter was transgender, and nothing would devastate me more than my daughter thinking that being herself in the world brought us sorrow. We must be clear about this with our children and with the world. The language we use and the way we share our stories teach others how to look at and know our children. Transgender children and youth are not reasons to be sad. They are the most joyful, inspiring human beings I have ever met. Still, it's not always easy.

After years of gender-nonconforming behavior, I watched my child get increasingly anxious. She struggled to cope with the world around her. She was distressed whenever she was grouped with boys at school or in activities. She stopped wanting to participate in activities she had previously enjoyed. She held it together at school and out in the world, but when she came home, she fell apart, exhausted from having had to act like everything was okay. We worked with professionals, read all the books on sensitive and anxious children, and equipped her with all the tools we could. We had a peace corner and glitter meditation jars. We took her to play therapy and occupational therapy. We read children's books that talked about feelings, gratitude, and emotional intelligence. We did yoga. Our bright and empathetic kid was struggling so deeply. Our entire life centered around supporting her emotional needs and managing from crisis to crisis. Eventually, depression joined the party. Nobody prepares you for a seven-and-a-half-year-old child who wants to die. It was the most difficult thing I've ever experienced. Watching my child hurt and not being able to fix it was heartbreaking and terrifying.

Over time, we were able to finally strike the right mix of support from therapy, coping skills we'd been giving her for years, and nutritional support to mitigate some underlying health issues. As she found some relief from the debilitating anxiety and depression, she also found a little space to unpack her identity. She began having conversations about gender and identity. She began to ask questions. As parents, we were relieved to see her suffering ease but uncertain where things were headed.

By the time she changed her name and pronouns and went out into the world as herself, it was so clear that this is who she was meant to be. Her light returned, and any lingering symptoms of anxiety and depression melted away. We had our kid back. It wasn't how we'd been expecting it to happen, but she wasn't struggling anymore. We were on this new and intense journey with no idea how to handle all the things—family, friends, school, church—but our kid was happy and thriving.

And there was sadness along the way. There were pangs of sorrow when we took down the family photos hanging on our walls that showed her before she transitioned. There were heavy moments when I wrapped up all the personalized Christmas ornaments that had her birth name on them and packed away her Christmas stocking with the same name. For me, there was even an odd sense of sadness around my outside-the-box, non-conforming kid transforming before my eyes to a gender-conforming dressed-head-to-toe-in-pink little girl. Some of that was nostalgia for what we had once known; some of that was grief and fear.

But any grief or fear that I or my partner experienced around our daughter's transition wasn't about her. Our fear was about the world. What would this mean for her future? Could we keep her safe? Parents don't dream of extra challenges for their children, and navigating the world as a transgender person is undoubtedly challenging. That's not because of who transgender people are but because of what they face in society. Our grief was that we had spent eight years of our child's life not knowing who she was. Our grief was about what we missed out on. For other parents, their grief may be about the dreams and plans they had for their child, who they'd hoped they would be in the world. Of course, like I talked about with gender reveals, we do that one to ourselves. I'm rarely one to give advice, but at every baby shower I attend, with every new parent I see, I want to beg them to stop planning their children's lives. If we could just stop putting our own expectations on these tiny humans who come into our lives, there would be so much more space for them to step into themselves and their futures.

## SUPPORT IN, PROCESSING OUT

A child doesn't transition alone. The whole family transitions, and everyone is going to have feelings about this. We must be careful and intentional about how we process those feelings. The circles of grief model can help guide us in these moments. The circles of grief are based on ring theory created by Susan Silk and Barry Goodman.[10] The idea is that in situations of crisis, loss, or grief, we put the person most impacted by the situation at the center of a series of concentric circles. If a friend experiences the loss of a spouse, we put that friend in a circle at the center, and then the people closest to them go in the next circle, and so on until we get to the outer circles, where maybe we put outside resource people or community members not directly impacted by the death. The idea is that support is directed inward while processing is directed outward. We don't want someone in an outer ring, like the neighbor who lives down the street, going to the widow, who would be in the center, for support.

When we're talking about a transitioning child, that child goes at the center of our circles. They don't need to help anyone else through their feelings. The hope is that only support is going in. The people in the circles surrounding the child are all available to help. The child is experiencing the most change. They are the most vulnerable. It doesn't mean the closest family members like parents and siblings aren't also experiencing change and vulnerability, but they are a circle removed from the center. Parents and siblings have the job of showing up in love and support for their child while finding people in outer circles with whom to process their feelings. Those feelings are valid and important; they just aren't the responsibility of the transitioning child. This may seem obvious as a theory, but there are subtle ways that parents put their grief or feelings on their child. Little comments about how carefully they chose their child's birth name or how much a parent loved that dress the child wore for a special occasion can deeply impact a child. We should process those thoughts and feelings with people who can appropriately listen and support us in moving through them.

This becomes true for every person in the child's life. As a family transitions together, many people come along for the journey. There are parents and siblings, and then there are grandparents, aunts, uncles, and cousins. From closest friends to neighbors and community members and everyone in between, each person will have their own experience of your child's transition. These folks aren't in the innermost circles but perhaps the circles just beyond that. They will have processing of their own to do, but it is not your job to help them through it. I encourage you to set boundaries, to point them toward resources and people in outer circles to help them process.

Every person and every family will be different, but if we communicate expectations, we are more likely to see those expectations met. In the same way your child cannot and shouldn't have to hold your grief, you cannot and shouldn't have to hold the feelings of every person around you. You need to be able to support your child first and foremost. This is far easier said than done, but take a moment to think through a strategy. Identify people who are or could be your strongest supporters. Maybe one of your siblings can help your parents process. Maybe your best friend can help educate and equip the rest of your friend group. It just can't always be you.

In the end, I always come back to this. We are a resurrection people. As Christians, we understand death and new life. We cannot get from Good Friday to Easter Sunday without going through Holy Saturday. There is waiting. There is sadness. There is fear. Our children do not die when they transition. They are finally able to live. Often what dies is so much of what we believed to be true and static in the world around us. Author, parent, and activist Glennon Doyle says, "First the pain, then the rising." That feels deeply true to my experience parenting a transitioning child.

# 5 | ACCEPTANCE IS PROTECTION

Over 40 percent of transgender people attempt suicide at some point in their life. That was the first statistic I learned as the parent of a transgender child. It wasn't an abstract number. It was my daughter. The hair on my arms stands up whenever I say it aloud. The number comes from a report from the American Foundation for Suicide Prevention and the Williams Institute,[1] which analyzed results from the 2011 National Transgender Discrimination Survey. It's just one of many alarming statistics about transgender people. Transgender and nonbinary people experience high rates of depression, anxiety, and suicidality.

The Trevor Project's 2022 National Survey on LGBTQ+ Youth Mental Health[2] gathered insights from nearly thirty-four thousand LGBTQ+ youth, ages thirteen to twenty-four, across the United States. Forty-eight percent of them were transgender or nonbinary. Fifty-three percent of transgender and nonbinary youth reported seriously considering suicide in the past year; that number rises to 59 percent when we look at Black transgender and nonbinary young people. Nineteen percent of transgender and nonbinary youth surveyed reported a suicide attempt. Seventy-eight percent of transgender and nonbinary youth reported symptoms of anxiety, and 65 percent reported symptoms of depression.

Sometimes people look at data like this and see it as confirmation that there is obviously something wrong with transgender people. Why else would they struggle so much? Proponents of this thinking often consider conversion therapy, sometimes lauded as "reparative" therapy, a viable option to "fix" not just transgender and nonbinary people but all LGBTQ+ people. Conversion therapy has been widely discredited and shown to be deeply harmful to those subjected to it. Twenty-six states have laws or regulations in effect protecting young people from the practice,[3] and it is widely opposed by all major medical and mental health associations.[4] According to the 2022 Trevor Project data, 22 percent of transgender and nonbinary youth were threatened with or subjected to conversation therapy. For LGBTQ+ youth threatened with or subjected to conversion therapy, it doubled their risk of a suicide attempt.

Transgender and nonbinary youth do not struggle because there is something inherently wrong with them or because they need to be fixed. They struggle because of what they face in the world. If we look at the same study from the Trevor Project, fewer than one in three transgender and nonbinary youth had homes that affirmed their identity. Fifty-eight percent of transgender and nonbinary youth wanted mental health care and were unable to access it. Seventy-one percent of transgender and nonbinary youth reported being discriminated against based on their gender identity, and 37 percent reported being physically threatened or harmed due to their gender identity. People living at the intersection of more than one marginalized identity will experience layers of impact as they navigate systemic barriers to their well-being and success. Black and brown transgender and nonbinary people are among those most at risk.[5]

A record number of anti-LGBTQ+ bills were introduced in state legislatures in 2022, with twenty-two being signed into law.[6] In the Trevor Project 2022 survey, 93 percent of transgender and nonbinary youth worried about transgender people being denied access to gender-affirming care, 91 percent worried about transgender people being denied access to the bathroom, and 83 percent worried about transgender people being denied the ability to play sports. Meanwhile, the youth surveyed reported lack of support at home, in school, and in their communities, all of which directly impacted their well-being. No wonder transgender people, especially young people, struggle. They are facing extraordinary hardship and vilification in the world today. Just turn on the news. Read the headlines. Transgender and nonbinary youth are supposedly threatening their peers on the sports field, girls in bathrooms, God in our churches, and everything for which this country stands.

There's a flip side to all that data, and we see it over and over again in studies. When transgender and gender-expansive youth are affirmed and supported in their identity, they have the opportunity to thrive. In the Trevor Project data, LGBTQ+ youth who reported having affirming homes, schools, and communities had a reduced risk of suicide. Research from the Family Acceptance Project[7] has shown that family acceptance is a significant protective factor for LGBTQ+ youth in the face of suicide, depression, and substance abuse. In fact, simply calling transgender people by their affirmed name reduces depression symptoms[8] and suicidal ideation. The TransYouth Project is the first large-scale, national, longitudinal study of socially transitioned transgender children to date. Its research[9] shows that transgender youth who are supported in their gender identity have levels of depression comparable to their cisgender siblings and peers and only mildly elevated levels of anxiety. Furthermore, data from study after study shows that access to gender-affirming medical care results in better mental health outcomes.[10] Conversion therapy is not the answer; support, affirmation, and access to care are the clear way forward.

What about faith? Religious faith is known to be a protective factor[11] for some young people when it comes to suicide. Even parental faith has been linked to lower suicide risk in teens, regardless of the young people's personal connection to religion.[12] Unfortunately, that doesn't seem to be the case for youth who aren't straight or cisgender. In fact, some studies show that LGBTQ+ youth raised in religious homes are at an increased risk for suicide.[13] A 2020 analysis by the Trevor Project[14] showed that religiosity had little impact on a young person's suicidality, but the incidence of parents using religion to say negative things about LGBTQ+ people was much more impactful.

This aligns with everything in this book so far: affirmation and acceptance protect gender-diverse young people. Being told that who they are is wrong causes harm. If faith is important to them or their family, it will cause even more harm to hear that the people they love think who they are is wrong. When any young person is told that who they are is not acceptable in the sight of God, the impact is devastating and long-lasting. Gender-diverse youth, like all youth, need to know they are loved and accepted unconditionally for who they are both by those closest to them and by the God who created them. When that happens, they are able to grow and thrive.

Let me say it again. There is nothing wrong with transgender and nonbinary people. Their suffering comes from a world that is built on their exclusion, marginalization, and oppression. We don't need to feel bad for them because they are somehow lacking; we need to love and celebrate them in the face of a world committed to doing otherwise. Even young people who are loved and supported by their families and communities are impacted by the world around them, by hyper-gendered expectations, by the changing political and legal landscape, and by a world that defines beauty with narrow masculine and feminine ideals. Beyond offering love and acceptance, we can help dismantle the systems that oppress them and all of us. Transgender and nonbinary people do not need to blend in or fit into the gender binary to be at peace. Like all of us, they are seeking congruence among their body, identity, and expression along with the ability to be themselves in the world without it constantly telling them they are wrong or less than.

## WHAT IF THEY CHANGE THEIR MINDS?

The data is compelling, and perhaps you're feeling ready to take the next steps in affirming your child's expressed gender identity. The next question I'm always asked is "But what if they change their minds?" First, we need to understand that transgender children who are persistent, consistent, and insistent in their gender identity do not often change their minds. Their gender is as stable as their cisgender peers', and we see that they behave like their cisgender peers of the same gender across various study measures.[15] In fact, when studied, transgender children are statistically indistinguishable from their cisgender peers.[16]

Data from the TransYouth Project suggests that children who transition do so because of their strong sense of their identity.

That is to say that they change their expressed gender because of their identity; they do not change their identity because of their gender. The data shows that supporting and affirming a gender-diverse young person does not change their identity, but it can save their lives. Giving young people the space to explore who they are in the context of a safe and loving home and community fosters confidence, security, and a sense of belonging that will serve them regardless of who they end up being.

Critics often point to those who have detransitioned as evidence that supporting a child in transitioning is ill-advised. *Detransitioning* is the language used by some to describe someone who, after their initial gender transition, returns to living as the gender that aligns with the sex they were assigned at birth. For example, if someone who was assigned female at birth transitions to live as the boy they know themselves to be and then returns to living as the girl everyone thought they were, people might say they detransitioned. The word *detransition* has become politically charged and weaponized against the community. Advocates are shifting the language they use to talk about these individuals, using words like *retransitioned* or talking about them having transitioned multiple times.

Meanwhile, data shows that the major factors in detransition align with the reasons we've already said transgender people struggle: what they face in society.[17] Specifically, studies note that social pressure, exposure to violence, discrimination, and family pressure are among the key reasons people detransition. The reasons are external opposed to internal. It breaks my heart to know that folks who have bravely sought to live as their true selves were met with so much resistance and harm, whether physical, emotional, or circumstantial, that they went back into hiding to survive. But we must be clear that those situations do not indicate that someone's identity is any less true or valid.

The concern is heightened with young people because people have a hard time understanding that transgender children know themselves just as well as cisgender children do. But the data continues to show just that. Dr. Kristina Olson of the TransYouth Project published data last year[18] showing that five years later, transgender study participants overwhelmingly maintained their identities. In the small percentage of youth who now identify as cisgender, it was most common for them to have initially socially transitioned before age six and transitioned again before age ten. This is important, and I'll explain why.

What happens to these young people who no longer know themselves to be transgender, even if they are a small population? Well, they retransition. They go back to living as the gender everyone thought they were based on the sex they were assigned at birth. Through the process, they will have walked closely with their family, community, and probably mental health practitioners. They will know they were loved unconditionally, trusted deeply, and supported in being what felt like their truest selves for that time. If the goal is to raise young people who know themselves, who develop self-trust and autonomy, I'd call that a success. It gets a little more complicated when medical transition begins, but that's why it's so significant that most of these young people who transitioned again did so before the age of ten. That's before any irreversible steps, and likely any steps at all, around a medical transition would have been taken. It's also why there is such care and caution when it comes to taking any medical steps, which we'll dive into shortly.

Another popular concern around transitioning youth, especially teenagers, is that it's a trend. Being transgender isn't a fad, and young people don't generally transition because of peer pressure. If we remember all the challenges that are a part of navigating the world as a transgender person, it's unlikely that any person claiming the identity because it's "what the cool kids are doing" would be willing to maintain the charade. In fact, when gender-diverse youth are bullied at higher rates than their peers, it's implausible to consider someone claiming to be transgender or nonbinary for the sake of social status or popularity. The ideas of both rapid-onset gender dysphoria and social contagion have been debunked.[19]

Our job is to love and support our kids. The best way to do that is to believe them when they tell us who they are, to affirm them, and to journey alongside them. In a 2018 *Canadian Family Physician* article[20] calling for a refocus on the health of transgender and gender-diverse children, the authors wrote, "Our main priority is not predicting children's adult identities; it is supporting children's present and future health and well-being." This is it. What if they change their mind? The answer is that it doesn't matter if they change their minds. I can't focus on or control who they are going to be, but I can focus on who they are right now. Building healthy, trusted, and connected relationships with our kids is the goal. Maybe your kid will need a new wardrobe or a new name. Maybe you will have to notify dozens of people that their gender has shifted again. Maybe you'll worry about what people think about you. Those things can bring up some real feelings, and you should talk to someone about them. Remember, we process out. We don't let our feelings, our shame, or our fear get in the way of doing right by our child. It's not about you. It's about the little one, or not-so-little one, who will know how much their parents respected them and were ready to do whatever necessary to support them.

So what do they need? What does acceptance look like? What is a gender-affirming approach? What does it mean to transition? Remember, when talking about transgender people, transitioning refers to the shift from living as the gender the world gave them to living as their true self. There are three main ways to transition: socially, legally, and medically.

## SOCIAL TRANSITION

First, there are social transitions. With young children, this is generally the only transition, although a legal transition can come soon after. A social transition means changing one's pronouns and often (though not always) their name so they can go out in the world as themselves. Sometimes it means a wardrobe change or redecorating a child's room. It involves layers of communication and education on the part of parents or guardians as they bring everyone in their child's life on board. There are conversations to be had with family, school, church, sports, and activities. It can feel intimidating and overwhelming, but in the next chapter, I'll share some of my favorite tools and guidance to help you on your way.

A social transition usually includes the act of coming out or sharing one's LGBTQ+ identity with loved ones or even the world. The general understanding of coming out as a momentous and singular point in time fails to recognize that coming out is something that LGBTQ+ people do repeatedly throughout their lifetime. Sometimes there is a clear and momentous first, but other times it's more gradual. That's true when a child transitions as well. A child may begin a social transition by using a different name and pronouns with their immediate family, for weeks or months, before then sharing that with widening circles of people. In teens, sometimes we see the opposite. They will share their identity and use new pronouns with their closest friends, but it can be some time before they share their identity with family. In addition to the nebulous nature of coming out, transitioning includes a variety of steps that individuals may or may not choose to take over a lifetime.

## LEGAL TRANSITION

Next, there are legal transitions. This can include legal name changes and changing gender markers on identification documents like birth certificates and passports. The rules and processes for each of these documents vary, but let's talk about why and when you might update these documents and where you can find the necessary information to do so. Legal documents can impact a child's ability to attend school as themselves and move through the world, without being misgendered or deadnamed, whether that's getting on a plane or going to the dentist.

The term *deadname* refers to a transgender person's birth name. To deadname someone is to use that birth name in opposition to their chosen or affirmed name. Doing so can jeopardize the physical and emotional safety of that individual, and it can even be seen as an act of violence. When someone is called by their birth name, they are reminded of the experience of having to be someone in the world who they are not. Deadnaming someone also has the potential to out them to people around them, which comes with its own risks. *Outing* is a term we use when someone else discloses a person's transgender identity, intentionally or unintentionally, without that person's permission. Whether done intentionally or not, the harm dead-naming causes is real.

Many transgender people face barriers to a legal transition including financial cost and the ability to navigate the bureaucracy of the system. However, some resources do exist to help families overcome those barriers. But before we get into any of that, let's talk about when you might choose to update these identity documents. The legal name change is usually the first step most families consider. This can be helpful in updating school records, medical office records, and everywhere that your child's name is used. The process varies a little bit state to state, so you'll need to consider what the requirements and procedures are in your state. My favorite resource for all identity document information is the National Center for Transgender Equality's Identity Document center (www.transequality.org/documents). You can click on various state or federal documentations and read current information about the change processes.

Once you file with the court for a name change, you may or may not have to attend a court hearing. You may also be required to publish your intent to change your child's name in the newspaper and then announce that it has been changed after you receive the formal name-change judgment. This practice is intended to prevent people from changing their names to escape creditors or other consequences of their bad actions. You can petition the court to waive this requirement and to seal the court documents, protecting your child's privacy. Some states have abolished this requirement, either just for minors or for all people. In most states, you can go through the name-change process without a lawyer's assistance; however, a lawyer with expertise in this area can ensure your child is as protected as possible now and in the future. Additionally, you will likely want to be certain of your child's chosen name. Many transgender and nonbinary youth try on quite a few names before one truly sticks. It can be a financial burden and legal hassle to change a name multiple times. Finally, most states will require all legal parents or guardians to be in favor of the name change.

We began our daughter's name-change process a little less than a year after she transitioned. Her name was stable, and she was anxious to have her name correct on everything including her health insurance card and her doctor's office records. It took us about four months from start to finish. At nine years old, she appeared before a judge with me and her father by her side. The judge was kind, and after we had satisfactorily answered his questions, he turned to Rebekah. He invited her up to bang the gavel herself and order us to take her to whatever restaurant she wanted. She banged the gavel with the biggest grin on her face and declared that we had to take her to Starbucks. When the barista asked her name, she proudly gave them her newly legal name so they could write it on the cup of her frozen, sugar-filled, coffee-free beverage.

Once you go through the process for a legal name change, you can update the name on all other identity documents including birth certificate, health insurance cards, any possible bank accounts, social security cards, driver's licenses, and passports. Meanwhile, the gender marker is separate from the name change. Your ability to update the gender marker on a child's birth certificate varies from state to state, with some states requiring nothing more than self-attestation, while others require medical documentation indicating the person has undergone surgery.

Still others don't allow for the gender marker to be changed at all. Fortunately, on a federal level, everyone can change the gender marker on their passport by simply filling out the appropriate forms. Beginning in 2022, the X gender marker option was added to the US passport meaning "unspecified" or "another gender identity"; however, the US State Department specifies it cannot guarantee that the X gender marker won't cause problems while traveling through countries that may not recognize such a marker.[21] Another concern is the level of scrutiny it could draw for transgender and nonbinary travelers, who already struggle with TSA screenings.[22]

The pieces of a legal transition can be overwhelming, and the policies and requirements change frequently. Organizations in many states across the country offer free or low-cost legal services to navigate these processes. Some examples include Trans Affirming Alliance in New Jersey and Transgender Legal Defense and Education Fund's Name Change Project based in New York but serving multiple states. You can ask your local LGBTQ+ community center for recommendations or check the resources in the back of the book for more information.

If you are unable or not ready to pursue these legal updates, you can support your child by advocating for them to be consistently and exclusively called by their affirmed name in all places. This takes persistence and insistence, but the impact is dually felt as the child avoids the experience of being called the wrong name as often as possible but also as they become aware of the way you are advocating for them. They may not know right away, and that's okay. Over time, they will see how hard you fought for them, and they will carry that with them always.

## MEDICAL TRANSITION

When it comes to gender-related care, gender clinics and individual practitioners across the country provide careful and professional evidence-based care to our children. Unfortunately, in many states, those practitioners and that care are in jeopardy thanks to legislative attacks. Nothing enrages me more than the idea that legislators who have never met my child and who have no medical training or expertise believe it is their right to determine what care my child should receive.

While the political debates rage, the fact is there are clear guidelines and best practices for treating our children. First and foremost, the following major medical associations have made clear their support of affirming medical care for transgender youth: the World Health Organization, the Endocrine Society, Pediatric Endocrine Society, the American Academy of Child and Adolescent Psychiatry (AACAP), the American Medical Association, the American Academy of Pediatrics (AAP), the American Psychiatric Association, and the World Professional Association for Transgender Health (WPATH).[23] These medical associations have published guidance regarding appropriate evidence-based clinical care for transgender and gender-diverse youth and released statements opposed to legislative attacks on said care.

Misinformation runs rampant around medical treatment for transgender children. I'm not a doctor, and best practices and guidelines may be updated after this book goes to print, but here is some basic information about the kinds of medical care available for and provided to transgender children. Prior to puberty, transgender children are treated with support, individual counseling, and family counseling. Beginning at Tanner Stage 2 of puberty, a child may be eligible for a hormone-blocking medication. These are generally delivered via injection or implant. These medications prevent a child from going through the puberty of the sex they were assigned at birth and developing the associated secondary sex characteristics.

For my daughter, this meant avoiding facial hair growth, the development of an Adam's apple, a deepening voice, and changes in bone structure. Those secondary sex characteristics would have been devastating to her. She would have felt like her body was betraying her despite the love, acceptance, and affirmation that surrounded her. Given what we went through prior to her transition and the things she has said since, I genuinely believe access to hormone-blocking medication to pause puberty saved her life. I don't know that she'd be here without it.

For transgender boys, hormone blockers prevent them from developing breasts and widening hips and beginning menses. For both transgender boys and girls, this prevents the associated dysphoria, or distress, of their body not matching who they know themselves to be. It can also prevent them from potentially wanting or needing other gender-affirming surgeries in the future (like chest masculinization or facial feminization procedures). For other youth who perhaps aren't yet clear and confident in their identity, hormone-blocking medications allow them to hit the pause button, giving them time to explore further without the added stress and potential trauma of puberty. If this medication is stopped, then puberty resumes as it would have prior to intervention.

The next possible medical intervention for a transgender youth is gender-affirming hormone treatment. For transgender girls, this means estrogen, and for transgender boys, it's testosterone. Nonbinary youth find the path that feels best for them. This allows young people to go through the puberty aligned with, or more closely aligned with, their affirmed gender. The specific age at which gender-affirming hormone treatment is introduced varies greatly based on the individual, the practitioner, and related circumstances, but it is generally not considered until the teenage years. This is the first transition-related care that will eventually result in irreversible changes, and as such, it is treated with the necessary care and caution.

Finally, some transgender people pursue gender-affirming surgical procedures including what we often refer to as top surgery (chest masculinization for men) or bottom surgery (vaginoplasty for women). It's important to know that these aren't the only transition-related surgical procedures. Others include things like breast augmentation, facial feminization procedures, phalloplasty, and more. There is no single surgery transgender people have to complete their transition, and many never undergo surgery at all. They are who they say they are prior to and regardless of any surgical intervention. Young people are not eligible for surgeries until later in their teens, and the specific circumstances depend on the specific surgery, the individual, and their individual health history.

None of these treatments is taken lightly. All of them require collaboration between mental health providers and medical providers. There is no set path for all transgender youth. These are individualized decisions made by multidisciplinary teams of clinicians in partnership with families and in accordance with medical guidelines. Insurance coverage of all these procedures varies greatly depending on your provider, although it is improving over time. Some insurance plans continue to exclude all gender-affirming care, although doing so may violate health care law prohibiting discrimination on the basis of sex among other things. For information about specific situations, contact LGBTQ+ advocacy organizations and legal professionals in your state.

You can find out what your plan covers by looking through your summary of benefits and plan coverage. Watch for language about exclusions related to transgender health care or "sex change" procedures. If your insurance plan is provided by an employer, you can advocate within your company for that coverage to be expanded. Generally, your human resources department can point you in the right direction. Without insurance coverage, and even sometimes with, gender-affirming care can be exorbitant and inaccessible. Some clinics throughout the country provide care based on a sliding financial scale or with grant support to aid in these situations, but more are always needed.

Much like the children's books of the same name, transitioning is a *Choose Your Own Adventure* experience. Some adults medically transition to gain the confidence they need to socially transition. Other people never medically transition because it's not something that feels right for them or because they do not have the resources to do so. The same goes with legal transition. Many transgender people lack identity documents that align with their gender identity due to the barriers they face when navigating the courts, potential financial constraints, and complicated bureaucratic systems. There is no single part of transition that makes a transgender person's identity valid. They are who they know themselves to be regardless of what steps they take to transition or whether they transition at all.

# 6 | WHAT NEXT?

Your head may be spinning as you take these steps with your child. You're shifting what you've understood to be true since likely before your child even came into this world. Take another deep breath. My friend Aubrey Thonvold, who serves as executive director for ReconcilingWorks, an organization that works toward the full inclusion of LGBTQ+ people in the Lutheran Church, is one of the most calming and grounded people I know. She does the often challenging but always sacred work of facilitating conversations and evolving policy and practice to create a church that more accurately reflects the kingdom of God. I say her work is challenging, and yet she explicitly coaches people to not describe this work as hard. She says that if we frame the conversation around how difficult the work is, how challenging the conversations will be, it will impact the energy we bring to the work and, in the end, our ability to make progress in that work.

As a queer person herself, she encourages folks who work in this space to gracefully engage with others, listening to their stories and their concerns, to perhaps find a way forward together. If we are at mile marker nineteen on this journey and the people we're talking to are at mile marker two, we can't expect them to skip the next seventeen miles. (Of course, we can and should set boundaries to protect our well-being and our children along the way. We'll talk in depth about this in the next chapter.) I think this is true for us too. Our kids may be many steps ahead of us, and we're desperately trying to catch up and bring everyone even farther behind us along for the ride. When I saw Aubrey present on the idea of graceful engagement at an inclusion symposium where I was speaking, I was inspired by her calm and embodied practice.

Everything we did started with our breath. She invited us to settle into our bodies. When we're feeling overwhelmed, it's so easy for our thoughts to run far ahead of the rest of us, but when we slow down, get quiet, and focus on our breath, we can think and feel more clearly. Aubrey encouraged participants to take a breath, make space, and then take a step. Those words have become an anchor for me. Breathe deep. Make space. Take a step. When we encounter challenges or questions in our journey, whether our own or those of the people we are educating, we breathe deep. Then we listen and learn from them, finding common ground. This helps us make space, and then we can take a step into that space we've created. We're not going to get ourselves or the people around us to the end of the marathon in a sprint, but we can take steps that feel good and grounded. When it gets to be too much, breathe deep, make space, and take a step. This chapter is filled with parent-to-parent resources and guidance on navigating the steps ahead with and for your child.

## MUSCLE MEMORY

Changing the pronouns you use with your child and the name you call them may be challenging at first. You have a lot of muscle memory stored, pushing you to do it one way. As I've said before, you don't have to get it all right immediately, but you do need to work at it. My best advice for this is to practice. Actually practice using their name and pronouns out loud as many times and in as many contexts as possible. Some parents fall into a habit of using the pronouns and name they are accustomed to and comfortable with when they are talking to other people *about* the child. It gives them a chance to relax a little from all the *trying*, and they think it's harmless. It's not. It reinforces the muscle memory you already have and erodes the work you're doing.

Commit to using your child's name and pronouns in all places at all times (unless, of course, there are some places where they don't want you to yet). That means, for instance, when you and your co-parent are discussing your child or your day after all the kids are in bed at night, you use your child's affirmed name and pronouns. It takes time to let it all sink into the deepest levels of your consciousness. You'll get there, and going all in is the fastest way to help you do so. I promise you, I can't imagine calling my daughter by her birth name or using male pronouns now. This is who she is, who she's always been, and it just took us a while to figure it out.

This is even more salient if your child finds themselves trying out different names and pronouns along the way. Sometimes it takes a couple names for one to stick. Sometimes they try on how different pronouns feel. It can feel pointless to get used to the name or pronouns of the day when you assume they'll change again, but it's part of accepting and living into who your child is telling you they are in real time. It impacts your ability to use those names and pronouns in front of them, which in turn impacts their confidence in your acceptance and support of them. Practice. Let them see how nonnegotiable this is for you. Make sure they know that wherever their path leads, you will be there, figuring it out, doing the work, and loving them out loud.

## DON'T DO IT ALONE

The learning curve is high for most of us when it comes to raising these kiddos. There is so much to learn, so much to process, and so much to share. You don't have to do any of it alone. In fact, you shouldn't do it alone. First, you'll be navigating this journey with the other parental figures in your child's life. This could include your partner, co-parents, or other guardians. You are going to need to communicate with one another. Supporting our kids through any significant life change can strain our relationships, and this certainly qualifies.

Prioritize these relationships by finding time to collaborate around your child and the work of parenting but also make time to nurture the other aspects of your relationship beyond co-parenting, if those exist. For instance, if you're in a romantic relationship or marriage, tend to that. Schedule time for connection, date nights, fun, or rejuvenation. Figure out who you can lean on to make that happen. If you and your co-parents are coming at your child's gender identity and expression from different places, seek help and seek community. Professional help includes therapists (individual, relationship, and family). There are folks who can help you navigate the family systems at play as well as offer expert insight and guidance as to what your child needs in that moment.

Find communities of people who understand what you're going through. Talking to and learning from other parents who are raising or have raised transgender and nonbinary children is perhaps the single most powerful thing you can do. We care so deeply for our children, and when everything we imagined for their future is flipped on its head, it can be scary. Parents who have been through what we are going through show us that things do get easier. Finding parents raising kids in a similar context can be powerful too—single parents, parents who share your racial or cultural background, parents living in a similar political context. The power of hearing so many people share similar experiences reminds us that we are not alone. This isn't hard because we're doing it wrong. It's just hard, and there is so much hope.

There are so many places to find this kind of community right now. Countless online support groups live on social media platforms like Facebook. One popular Facebook group for moms is called Serendipitydodah, home of the "mama bears" (www.realmamabears.org). This community is predominantly for mothers of LGBTQ+ kids, but there are also subgroups specifically for parents raising transgender and gender-expansive young people. Other Facebook groups specifically cater to dads as well as all parents. National organizations like PFLAG have local chapters providing the opportunity to connect with other parents and family members in person and/or online depending on the area. LGBTQ+ community centers and local health care providers also host groups or can point you to resources in your area. There are too many options available for you not to take advantage of them.

The first time I stumbled into a Facebook group for parents of transgender children, I remember tentatively introducing myself and explaining that I wasn't sure if I belonged there just yet or if I would ever but that we were following our kid's lead. People welcomed and affirmed me, and then I started reading through posts. Post after post, I read stories of parents like me and kids like mine. Parents who were doing their very best, learning as fast as they could, and loving the kid right in front of them. I cried tears of relief because I knew, at that moment, that I had found my people. All these years later, that group is far bigger than it was when I joined, but I am still in connection with some of those first people with whom I interacted. We cheer each other on, we love each other's kids, and we fight for a world where all kids can be themselves. Now, when I hit a point in my parenting journey where I don't know what's next, where there are questions I can't answer (and yes, that still very much happens), I go to that group or others like it. I ask parents of kids who are older than mine, who have navigated things like dating and decisions about surgery, whose children are married and off living on their own, because those parents know what I don't know yet, and their kids are the continual possibility models for my kid's future. When I get scared, they remind me the kids are alright, and there is so much good in store for them.

## POSSIBILITY MODELS

I like the term *possibility models* instead of *role models*, at least in this context. It's not so much about telling our children who they should be or what they should grow into, but instead it's about what's possible. Thriving transgender and nonbinary young adults and adults show us what's possible for our children. I know my own daughter serves as a possibility model for kids, teens, and their parents from all over the country. As a public figure, an outspoken advocate, an author, an athlete, and a teenager who is living her fullest life, Rebekah inspires, but Rebekah also looks up to so many others, those who paved the way for her to live the life she does.

Sarah McBride, the first transgender person to speak at a Democratic National Convention, is a possibility model. Former press secretary for the Human Rights Campaign, Sarah became the highest-ranking elected transgender person in the United States in 2021 when she was elected to the Delaware State Senate. Chase Strangio, a lawyer for the ACLU fighting relentlessly (I will not say *tirelessly* because I know he is tired) for the rights of transgender children and youth, is a possibility model. Imara Jones, an award-winning journalist and the founder of TransLash media, tenaciously telling the stories of trans people to save trans lives, is a possibility model. Powerful and positive transgender people in the public eye show youth what's possible. Activists, writers, athletes, actors, and leaders like Schuylar Bailar, Raquel Willis, Josie Totah, Elliot Page, Zaya Wade, Laverne Cox, Nicole Maines, Tiq Milan, and Alok Vaid-Menon show teens a world where transgender people positively impact current events and culture.

Our children need to see what's possible for them. They need to see positive representation of people like them in every possible area of their lives. They need to know transgender authors, doctors, lawyers, elected officials, actors, and more. They need to know that who they are doesn't need to hold them back, and while the world might not be as ready for them as we wish it was, it's getting more so every single day. We can bolster our young people's self-esteem, self-concept, and resilience by connecting them to transgender and gender-expansive possibility models. We can ensure our homes are overflowing with positive representation of transgender people in books, shows, movies, social media, and more.

## IN-PERSON CONNECTIONS

Media representation and powerful, positive public figures who happen to be transgender are awesome, but our kids can also benefit from the real-life community that we ourselves need. As wonderful as it is to see people *out there* who have similar back-grounds to us, knowing people *right here* is also important. Many schools have affinity groups for LGBTQ+ students. LGBTQ+ community centers sometimes host groups for transgender and gender-expansive youth and teens.

Still, sometimes we can't find the resources and community we need in our local area. In this case, conferences and camps can be a lifesaver. Prior to the COVID-19 pandemic, gender con-ferences met regularly across the country and were places where young people could connect with their peers, parents could con-nect with each other and resource providers, and professionals could get much-needed professional development and network-ing. Post-pandemic, this is a little trickier, but it's still out there. Gender Spectrum, Philadelphia Trans-Wellness Conference, and Gender Odyssey are a few to look into.

Beyond conferences, there are camps designed for and dedicated to our kids. Transgender and nonbinary youth travel from all over the country to attend Harbor Camps, programs exclusively for them, in New Hampshire. The Naming Project is a faith-based camp for queer youth and allies each summer in Minnesota. Many other camps and conference centers have spe-cialty weeks that are geared specifically to LGBTQ+ campers. Just as powerful, some camps not exclusively for LGBTQ+ youth integrate gender inclusivity so deeply into the fabric of who they are that they consistently attract gender-diverse campers and staff. Camp Stomping Ground is one of those camps. Nestled in the Catskills, not far from Saratoga Springs, New York, Camp Stomping Ground is a container for community rooted in radi-cal empathy and restorative justice that has become home to transgender, nonbinary, and gender-expansive campers and staff year after year. Lutheran Outdoor Ministries of the Evangelical Lutheran Church in America (ELCA) is in the midst of a major initiative to become more inclusive of LGBTQ+ people, people with disabilities, and BIPOC people. People all over the country, in all areas of expertise, are working to create safer and more inclusive spaces for kids like ours.

I'm especially encouraged and inspired by the work organizations that do not cater specifically to the LGBTQ+ community are doing to become more inclusive of LGBTQ+ people. Our children cannot live their lives in specialty programs. We don't want them isolated from their peers. Being transgender or gender diverse is just one piece of who they are. We need organizations and spaces of all kinds that are safe and welcoming for our children. Pay attention to who is doing the work and how they are doing it. They will be your partners not only in raising the child in front of you but also in building a world in which they can continue to thrive.

## BOOKS

I mentioned books when we talked about possibility models, but let's dig a little deeper. When Rebekah transitioned, there were so many people to tell. One by one, we had to explain to people something that only sort of made sense to us. We had to be the experts in Rebekah's life, and that was tricky. We quickly realized people didn't need an actual primer on all things transgender. Instead, they needed a point of access. They needed a simple explanation and basic language. Cue children's books. These simple picture books gave us language and an outside voice to explain to folks what we already knew—being transgender wasn't actually complicated. Sure, the world is complicated for transgender people, but being transgender is just about who you are at your core being different from who the world thinks you are.

We ordered a copy of *I Am Jazz* by Jazz Jennings and Jessica Herthel. Rebekah already had a connection to Jazz. She watched a video of a young Jazz Jennings when I explained the word *transgender* to her. She felt seen in a way she had never before. Now, equipped with Jazz's picture book, Rebekah was able to read a story with her cousins and her grandparents and explain that she was just like Jazz. Rebekah may have been doing something hard and new, but she wasn't doing it alone. Jazz was with her.

Later, Rebekah would start a new school as herself. She'd make new friends who only knew her as Rebekah. She'd try to tell her new best friend about being transgender, and that friend would not believe her. It didn't make sense. Rebekah was just Rebekah. How could she have ever been anything else? After some awkward messages with the parents and a lot of breath holding on our part, we sent a copy of *I Am Jazz* home with this friend to read with her parents so she could better understand Rebekah's story.

There's something deeply validating about being able to point to a story in a book and say, "That's just like me." It's in print. It's real. It's not just in my head. It helps us feel less alone to know that stories like ours live in the pages of books on the shelves of our local libraries and bookstores. It helps us *know* we aren't alone. Similarly, when our family and friends read these books, they can see our story as a part of a larger fabric.

As adults who care about transgender children and youth, I encourage you to read the stories of transgender adults because as much as we love our children and as well as we know them, those of us who are not transgender do not share that piece of our children's lived experiences. The transgender adults in my life—in person, in the pages of books, and in stories told on screens of all kinds—have been my greatest teachers and have made me a better parent to my child.

But when it comes to beginning to teach the people in our circles about our children, I adore picture books. I read them and gift them to children, families, and adults. They are bite-size, accessible points of entry into what it means to be transgender and what it means to love the transgender child in front of you. You can find a list of some of my favorite books sharing stories that feature transgender people of all ages in the resources at the back of the book, including many written by transgender people.

## SCHOOL

We had the unique gift of homeschooling the year Rebekah transitioned. It is something I can only describe as a God thing. My children had attended a lovely little nature-based Montessori school from the time they were toddlers, and at the end of Rebekah's first-grade year, we decided we wanted to take a break from that, but we didn't feel like public school was the next right step. So despite having sworn I would never do so, I found myself homeschooling my older two children for kindergarten and second grade. That year was an intense time of discovery, learning, and healing. Homeschooling gave us space we wouldn't have otherwise had. I'm not suggesting you need to homeschool your kids while they transition, but it just happened to be a part of our journey.

Rebekah transitioned in April that year, and by the time August rolled around, I felt called to enroll our kids in public school. Things had stabilized a bit in our life with Rebekah step-ping confidently into her identity and our family bringing those around us on board. We knew Rebekah thrived in structured environments with peers, and we felt like we were in a place to help our school district figure out how to support a transgender student. To our knowledge, there was only one other transgender student in the district, and they were in high school. This was going to be a little different. We were also confident that if this didn't go well, we could pull her from school and continue home-schooling or pursue other options. That was a recurring notion for us as we navigated her transition. We were prepared to edu-cate and equip those around us to support her, and we were also prepared to cut and run from any situation where harm would come her way. That was part privilege and part commitment.

We came to the decision to enroll my kids in public school about a week before the school year was set to begin. The Holy Spirit can be quite pushy sometimes. I'll never forget the day I walked into Rebekah's future school, armed with a thick packet of information and resources about supporting transgender stu-dents, and said, "I need to enroll my child for school. I also need a meeting with the principal, and I'm going to need him to read this first." I had no idea how it was going to go, but remember, we were prepared to do whatever we needed to do to keep her safe. The meeting went surprisingly well. The school administra-tors didn't have a lot of knowledge, but they were willing to listen to us and learn from us about what our daughter would need to be safe and successful in school. Then they asked, "Well, what bathroom will she use?" My husband and I looked at each other. We knew this is where it might go all wrong. I said definitively, "She's a girl; she uses the girls' bathroom." The words echoed in my head as I waited for the response. "That makes sense," the principal responded. He was right. That does make sense.

Things went as well as they could, but we were still nervous waiting for school to start. The day before school started, someone knocked at our door. People didn't usually show up at our house without us expecting them; we had three children ranging in age from one to eight years old, so you never really knew what you were going to get if you surprised us. With the littlest child propped on my hip, I opened the door. There stood our school district's superintendent. He introduced himself, and he said he'd heard about our daughter. He went on to tell us that he would do everything he could to protect her. Her birth certificate with her legal name would be kept securely to ensure her privacy. The school's databases would all reflect her affirmed name. He kept talking, while I stared in disbelief. Finally, he said, "And if there is anything else you ever need, you let me know right away. If there is a problem, we will handle it. You have my word." I mumbled words of gratitude, closed the door, and the tears came. Relief. We weren't the only ones who would be fighting for our daughter.

Your experience with schools will vary greatly based on what part of the country you're in, what type of school you're attending, and the individual educators and administrators involved. Antidiscrimination laws vary state to state, and policies vary district to district. So the first thing you'll want to do is figure out what the laws are in your state and what the policies are in your district. These laws and policies change often, for better and for worse. Next, equip yourself with best practices and educational resources for your district. Finally, if there are LGBTQ+ community support organizations nearby, they may have direct experience or educational advocates who can help you in this process.

You may not have a superintendent who shows up at your door; most people don't. But there will be people who will advocate for your child. Find them and keep them close.

Some of the things you'll want to address with the school include what name your child will use (and if it's different from the name on their birth certificate, how that will be reflected in school databases), what facilities they'll use (bathrooms and locker rooms), to whom you want this information about their identity communicated, and what you'll do if issues arise with their peers or in the community. There are comprehensive gender support plans put together by multiple organizations to help you and the school in covering everything. Tools to help with these steps are available in the resources at the end of this book.

Rebekah's success in school depended both on the school's willingness to listen to and learn from us but also on our commitment to communicating clearly and consistently with them. In the early years, we communicated with her teacher, the school nurse, and her guidance counselor. For the most part, Rebekah being transgender was a nonissue in her day-to-day life. She was a girl, and that was that. But at the same time, we needed to know everyone was on the same page if concerns arose. We also needed Rebekah to know whom she could talk to without having to go through the process of outing herself or explaining to the adult she was seeking help from that she was transgender.

As she got older, we navigated things like gym class, puberty and sexual education in health classes, and athletics. With each new thing, we'd talk with Rebekah and follow her lead. As she entered middle school, she didn't need every teacher to know about this part of her, but she was on board with informing the principal and the guidance counselor so she knew she had people in her corner. Open communication is critical. Transgender and nonbinary students are disproportionately at risk of bullying, harassment, and assault compared to their cisgender peers.[1] Parents and educators cannot solve problems they don't know exist. Ensuring your child has safe access to someone they trust when they need support is critical to their success.

Finally, you can advocate for your schools to become safer and more welcoming spaces for transgender and nonbinary students. Do they have a Gender-Sexuality Alliance (GSA) or other club geared toward the acceptance and celebration of LGBTQ+ youth? Do they avoid separating students by gender, including for things like puberty education? Do they provide comprehensive sexual health education that is gender inclusive? Do they include representation of people of diverse gender identities and expressions in the classroom materials and curriculum? Are there clear policies around harassment, intimidation, and bullying related to gender identity and/or gender expression? Are the dress codes nongendered and inclusive of all types of expression? Do they ask for students' pronouns and make space for students and staff who don't fit within the binary?

This is ongoing work, and even schools committed to this work will still have places they can improve. The binary systems and expectations of gender are so entrenched in us that even those of us doing this work diligently as individuals can discover places where we trip on old beliefs. Our institutions will absolutely do the same. Rebekah ran into this in a ninth-grade biology class. A question on a quiz asked, "What are your chromosomes?" They were studying genetics, and the teacher thought this was a tangible way to check for comprehension. Unfortunately, Rebekah found herself not knowing how to answer. This particular teacher didn't know Rebekah was transgender, nor was there any reason the teacher needed to know. Rebekah had to decide whether she wrote XY, which, while honest, would be marked wrong by the teacher, who assumed she was cisgender. Then she'd have to out herself as transgender to the teacher to get the question corrected. Or she could lie and write XX. That answer would be marked correctly, and she could go on her way. Rebekah's friends got to the question on the quiz and looked over at her anxiously because they immediately knew this was a problem.

The fact is unless we have had genetic testing, we're all assuming what our chromosomes are anyway. People with genetic variations and intersex traits are more common than most of us realize. The world is more complicated and diverse than any of us were initially taught to believe. Our teaching must reflect that for the sake of all students. I'm sure you want to know Rebekah answered the question. There's a part of me that wants to say it doesn't matter. What matters is that she was asked a question that she shouldn't have been asked. That's what I want to tell the world, but parent to parent, she gave the answer the teacher wanted. It was marked correct. The teacher assumed Rebekah's sex chromosomes were XX, and so that's what Rebekah wrote. As much advocacy as she does in the world, she didn't want to have to out herself in science class to save her GPA.

When I found out, I asked Rebekah what she wanted me to do. This is something I've learned over the years. My instinct is to sound the alarms, educate the people, and solve all the problems. I can't imagine that comes as a surprise to you by now. When faced with a problem, I'm a full-speed-ahead kind of person. While that may be what I want to do in any given situation, it's not always what Rebekah wants. So I always defer to her. In this situation, she asked me to not contact her teacher. She didn't want to be outed. She agreed to let me contact the district to help them understand the problem to hopefully prevent other students from experiencing what she did as long as I ensured they wouldn't out Rebekah to her teacher. That's what I did.

I reached out to administrators, explained what had happened, and offered a resource, www.genderinclusivebiology .com, created and maintained by three science teachers helping educators understand how to be accurate and inclusive in science education without sacrificing the scope or age-appropriateness of the content. The administrator in charge of curriculum and instruction was grateful to be aware of what had happened and was already aware of the resource I provided. He said he had shared it with all district science teachers previously, but he realized he needed to share it again and do further education around the need. Sometimes it takes time and repetition for the resources, information, and standards of practice to trickle down through a system. It's good to remember for all kinds of places; even if there are good policies in place, it doesn't mean everyone is up to date with their implementation. And that's understandable; for instance, teachers are chronically overwhelmed and undersupported. Still, we need to continue to educate and advocate for the protection of all students when possible. But if it involves your own child, ensure you have their consent to proceed. It is their story, their identity, and their school.

## HEALTH CARE

Rebekah came home from school on a Friday afternoon with searing pain in her throat and a rising temperature. I was certain she had strep, but our family doctor's office was about to close. So I drove her to an afterhours clinic in a nearby town. I filled out all the paperwork while my increasingly lethargic child clung to my side. She was the kind of sick where her eyes were glassy, and she was slow to respond. She pitifully whimpered whenever I disturbed her by moving my arm to scribble my way through the forms on the clipboard I was holding. They called us back, and I was relieved to get things moving so I could get her medication and take her home to rest.

The nurse practitioner looked at the paperwork. She confirmed lots of details like our insurance, her birth date, and her primary care doctor. She got to the medication section and paused. "What's Supprelin?" I explained that it was a hormone-blocking medication delivered via a small implant in her arm. She looked confused. "Well, what's that for?" Rebekah looked at me with a look that begged me to move things along. She was so sick. She just wanted a strep test and to go home. I explained that Rebekah is transgender, and the medication helps prevent her going from the puberty she was assigned at birth. The nurse's brow furrowed. "She's transgender? You mean she wants to be a boy?"

I had to continue to explain to this medical professional that my daughter did not want to be a boy. She was a transgender girl, and she'd been living as herself for four years at that point. She needed a strep test and antibiotics so she could feel better. We got there eventually. She was positive for strep, and after twenty-four hours on antibiotics, she was on her way to recovery. But that didn't erase the fact that while she was trying to get basic medical care for something completely unrelated to her gender, she had to wait while her mom educated the medical practitioner about what it means to be transgender, why she was taking the medications she was taking, and that none of this was a factor in her very real strep infection.

And that was a fairly benign, if frustrating, interaction. Other transgender people experience this and far worse while trying to get care from primary care physicians, emergency room doctors, and more. For some trans people and their families, the challenges they face in trying to receive adequate medical care are compounded by racism, misogyny, ableism, and anti-fat bias. The urgent care they need is delayed or even denied because of their transgender identity. At the time of that visit, we had an affirming family doctor and a wonderful practice for gender-related care. I was taken by surprise when I needed to educate the practitioner in front of me, but I shouldn't have been. It wasn't the first time, and it wouldn't be the last.

I've had extensive conversations with a phlebotomist while getting my own blood drawn about "how horrible it is that they're doing gender surgeries on little kids." (She walked away with a very different perspective.) Prior to my daughter's name change, I've had to convince dentists that I wasn't trying to give them the insurance card for the wrong child because the name on the card didn't match the little girl standing in front of them. Parents often need to educate the health care practitioners we interact with on an occasional basis, and we need to be diligent in finding practitioners willing to educate themselves for our children's ongoing care. Whether it's their pediatrician, their therapist, or their dentist, our children need clinicians who understand what it means to be transgender.

## BREATHE

If you've made it this far, it might feel like once these kids of ours go out into the world being themselves, we must spend all our time running in front of them, or sometimes behind them, trying to make sure every place and person is ready for them. And that's kind of exactly what happens. Until there are proactive policies and adequate education in all places and in all areas that impact a child's life, this is what parents will need to do. It's all so our children can just be themselves, and it's worth it. But it's still a lot. Whatever you're feeling, notice it. How does it feel in your body? Don't judge it. It's all valid. Maybe take a few more deep breaths. Remember, none of this is a prescription. It's not a giant to-do list. Take what sounds helpful; leave what isn't. Our journeys share a lot in common, but they're also each unique.

I'm sitting in the corner of a bustling coffee shop writing these words. I wish you could be here with me. I wish we could sip lattes and share stories. I wish I could see your shoulders start to creep up with tension so I could remind you that it's going to be okay. You don't have to have it all figured out right now. I wish you could hear my voice catch in my throat and notice when I'm surprised by the tears that well up, even after all this time, as I share the things I've learned along this bumpy road. So much of it can feel practical and matter-of-fact, but there's emotion stored in my body from every step of the journey. It sneaks up on me. Maybe it will for you too. Remember: breathe deep, make space, take a step. If we ever get the chance, please know I'm always up for a latte and a hug. We're in this together.

# 7 | LOVING BOUNDARIES

Not all of us will have the right words to respond when we learn that our child is transgender. Some of us may struggle in the moment; others may struggle longer. That goes for the other people in our child's life too. There are a few things we can do to keep our children safe and best equip those around us to join us on this journey. Perhaps the first thing to consider is how we share the news with the people around us. With close family members and friends, some may want to share the news in person, while others might offer something in writing. And then you have church, school, activities, teachers, and coaches to consider. There isn't a singular right way to do any of this, but here are some things to consider.

While grand announcements can be tempting for the relief of it all being out in the open and everyone having the same information, these public declarations can also invite a level of drama and debate that isn't always helpful or necessary. For example, we specifically avoided a big announcement when we navigated Rebekah's transition with our church. Instead, we had a conversation with the congregational leadership about Rebekah's transition, let them know we were available as ongoing resources, and asked them to spread the word. We kind of put the church rumor mill to work for us. This allowed people the opportunity to receive this information in their own time, have their own initial reactions and even their second reactions, ask questions of each other or look stuff up, and talk to us when they were ready. This slow drip of information, if you will, was easier for them to acclimate to than a big announcement that everyone received at once. It allowed those who had received the information sooner and were in a different place in processing to help those who were having their initial reactions. It also prevented the community as a collective from taking people's first feelings and turning them into a bigger issue.

Along the lines of avoiding big announcements, there is also no need to notify every parent in any class or activity in which your child participates. You do not need to justify yourself or your child. Teachers can explain to students with simple verbiage like "Danny goes by Danielle now and uses she/her pronouns." Sometimes providing additional information to parents that they can discuss with students can be helpful, but any information shared about your child should be on your and your child's terms. There is nothing wrong with your child. Their being transgender is just a part of their life. Most importantly, however you share the news, make sure you have your child's consent and that they are a part of your plan. It is, after all, their identity. Your child determines when they are ready to share their identity and with whom.

## CLEAR IS KIND

When Rebekah transitioned and we shared the news with others, we had two rules for people to follow. First, they needed to use her affirmed name and correct pronouns; that meant calling her Rebekah and using *she* and *her*. Second, they could not ask

Rebekah questions about her identity, or ask anyone else questions about her identity, in front of Rebekah. We didn't expect everyone to be on board right away. We knew they'd have questions, even concerns or reservations, and we wanted to create space for them. Boundaries allowed us to do that.

Boundaries and clear expectations are critical tools for keeping your family safe while allowing you to live in community, to live in the world. For some people, these boundaries look like cutting every person out of your life who isn't waving transgender Pride flags and celebrating your child, privately and publicly, from the start. I understand this instinct, and you will need to do what feels right for you, but in my experience, raising my own child and working with families all over the country, sometimes the people around us need time. They care deeply for us and our children, and so they have questions. They're confused by the information and misinformation they're receiving from the world—the headlines, the news segments, the political rhetoric— as well as their prior understanding of both your child and people who are transgender or gender diverse. Many of these people who are unsure will come around. Some of them will become you and your child's biggest cheerleaders. Boundaries are a way to protect the most vulnerable, your child, while offering grace to those who don't understand for the sake of relationships and for the sake of growth.

Some people really struggle with boundaries. People-pleasing is deeply ingrained in us, and certain family dynamics discourage any type of boundary setting or asserting of independence. There is also a societal expectation, especially for women, that we should make the people around us comfortable. If the idea of boundaries feels icky to you or you're worried about hurting people's feelings by upholding boundaries around your child's transition, please know that boundaries are an act of love. They allow us to remain in community with people whom we otherwise might have to remove from our lives. Have you ever heard the saying "clear is kind"? Clearly articulating what you need from the people around you gives those involved guardrails for future interactions, keeping everyone safer than they'd be without them.

For us, a basic understanding of and willingness to follow our two rules was the ticket to being a part of our lives. It was nonnegotiable. Of course, people slipped up in the beginning. So did we. That was okay. But they had to be honestly and earnestly trying for us to allow them around our child. She was in a bubble at the center of our lives, and we only allowed support, love, affirmation, and celebration to permeate that bubble.

The circles of grief theory we talked about in a prior chapter is helpful again here, illustrating how support moves toward the inner circle, and processing moves out. Remember, the gender-diverse child is at the center. All support goes in; all processing goes out. Parents experience all sorts of emotions—fear, grief, loss, and anxiety—when their child is gender diverse. Those feelings are real and valid, but they are not the child's responsibility. Instead, parents can reach outward to trusted family and friends as well as affirming pastors, therapists, and support groups. This applies for each layer of the circle. Support in; processing out. The same theory that guides us in processing our own emotions allows us to navigate the many spaces in our child's world.

For us, this meant navigating conversations with everyone who was in relationship with our child and weighing their ability to learn, our capacity to teach them, and the value of their place in our lives. So close family members who needed some time and guidance? Yep. We committed that energy. We deeply valued our relationships with them, and we took the steps we needed to protect Rebekah while they learned. The dance school she attended? Nope. Their attitude when Rebekah transitioned was harmful to Rebekah despite our efforts to maintain our basic guidelines, and their place in our lives wasn't important enough for us to commit the energy to trying to help them grow and learn. We found a new dance studio that enthusiastically welcomed her and quickly became like family to us.

Other situations aren't as straightforward. A dear friend of mine from the mommy group I joined when I was pregnant with Rebekah struggled with Rebekah's transition. For me, this one was a yes. I valued her friendship deeply, and she was outwardly respectful of Rebekah while navigating her own personal and religious beliefs about transgender people. But sometimes a person's willingness to learn and grow hits its limit. Despite years of walking with our family on this journey, that friend eventually ended our friendship because she couldn't reconcile her own beliefs about the world with our family's choices. The end of that friendship was devastating to me, and yet I don't regret the years I spent on this journey with her. She was someone I valued greatly, and Rebekah was always safe. Sometimes we hope and believe people can learn and grow in ways for which they are simply not ready. As long as we don't sacrifice our child's well-being or our own in the process, we will still experience the pain and loss, but we will be rooted in our truth and integrity when we do.

The work of maintaining boundaries and ensuring the people around our child are reasonably safe people isn't work that ended after our daughter's initial transition. This is work that parents of transgender and gender-diverse children do for their whole lives. We become excellent detectives, doing deep dives on everyone from our children's teachers and coaches to their friends' parents and neighbors. Every interaction with a new person means trying to figure out where they stand. I scour social media for red flags. I gather clues in everything from the bumper stickers on people's cars to the election signs outside their homes. I listen closely to the way they talk about what's going on in the world today or how they describe their children. Is it filled with gendered expectations and assumptions? I look earnestly for signs of allyship and support—little rainbow stickers, posts during Pride month, or references to queer family members.

None of these can give me the whole picture, but as I do everything I can to not place my child into unsafe situations, I grasp onto these clues for dear life. My kids joke that I'm a creeper or that I'm really good at stalking people, but the reality is this finely tuned skill of learning everything I possibly can about a person or an organization is a desperate attempt to keep my family safe. This experience of hypervigilance isn't unique to parents of transgender and gender-expansive children. In fact, for people raising Black and brown children who continue to face bias, hate, and violence in the world, this is just a normal part of parenting. It's the reality they've always known. Parents of neurodiverse children and children with disabilities have to be hypervigilant as well.

## DISCLOSURE

Families with transgender and gender-diverse children also face decisions around how much they share about their story and with whom they share it. It is important for these families to know they can and should keep things private, things that are only theirs, for the sake of their child now and in the future. Sometimes people who have misinformed opinions about, and a lack of understanding around, being transgender believe that our children's identities and their stories are for public consumption, with or without their consent. We see this in the urge for parents to want to be notified if there are transgender children in their child's classes or activities or, worse, when they want to be given the option to opt their child out of being grouped with a transgender child. We also see this in the probing and invasive questions people ask about our child's experience for their own gratification or so that they can judge the validity of our child's identity. Other times, the urge to share comes from families who feel like they need to show people everything, and I mean everything, to justify their child's identity and their experience or to change hearts and minds.

Let me be absolutely clear here. Your child's identity and their experience are not up for debate. Your child's story is theirs and theirs alone. Transgender and gender-diverse people and their families do not owe anyone intimate details of their lives. Things like birth names, medical details, and private conversations don't need to be shared with the wider community. Less is more. It is not our job to use our child's personal lived experiences to convince others that our parenting choices are valid and good or that transgender people are worthy of love and belonging. It is our job to protect our children's privacy and their story.

When you're in the midst of your child's initial transition and doing the work of telling everyone your child knows that they go by a different name and/or pronouns, it can be hard to imagine, but eventually your child will just get to be themselves in the world. They will go new places and meet new people who never knew them by their birth name or the pronouns they used to use. They won't be the kid who used to be called [birth name] but goes by [affirmed name]. Rebekah is just Rebekah, and she has been for a long time now. This is a beautiful and holy thing, but it also brings up new questions and decisions.

To whom do you disclose that your child is transgender, when, and why? There aren't one-size-fits-all answers. Your decisions will depend on your child's age, maturity, and the kinds of spaces they inhabit. The decisions will certainly include your preferences as their parent, but I invite you to heavily prioritize their preference given that the identity is theirs alone. We should think twice before we demand our children disclose their transgender status to someone as a requirement to a relationship, any kind of relationship. That may feel uncomfortable to us as parents who are responsible for our child's well-being, but it is our child's identity, not our own. They must develop autonomy around and authority over that identity. Collaboration and caution are key.

I imagine you're thinking to yourself, *Isn't that a little hypocritical? You're writing a book about your kid.* I'm so glad you thought that because this is important. I am not telling you everything. I'm not sharing the conversations and stories that I have chosen to keep just for myself or those that Rebekah has asked that she keep for herself. She will be sixteen years old when this book goes to print, and she will have read every word. She has affirmed and approved of every anecdote that appears in these pages. And to be honest? I still worry. Because she is sixteen years old. Perhaps when she is twenty-six or thirty-six, she will wish these stories weren't in print.

I've tried to proceed with as much caution and as much of a "less is more" approach while honestly representing our experiences, but I won't know if it was enough for years to come.

Honestly, our situation would likely be different if I knew what I know now when she transitioned at eight years old or even before that. I held lots of things for myself, for her, for our family, but I also shared a lot. I am grateful I was as careful as I was, and I still wish there were things I handled more tenderly. We will talk more about this when it comes to what it means to advocate for your child and the wider community of transgender and nonbinary children and youth. But for now, I offer caution. Keep things close. Write them down. Cherish the intimate conversations that come with navigating this journey alongside your child. Protect their privacy, their struggles, and their joys with everything you have so that when they are grown, they don't discover that things they believed to be personal, vulnerable, and intimate were public knowledge whether through conversation or social media.

## LURID VERSUS HOSPITABLE CURIOSITY

You need to be adamant and firm in these boundaries because the world—from close personal friends to strangers—will ask you to divulge everything for their own benefit. It's not quite as nefarious as it sounds; it's human nature. When talking about the inclusion of people who are different from us, it is important to talk about curiosity. I first learned this concept through ReconcilingWorks,[1] and it is now integral to my work.

There are two kinds of curiosity. Hospitable curiosity helps us better show up in community with one another. It is curiosity that seeks to understand the needs of another. We are leaning into hospitable curiosity when we reach out to anticipated guests for a dinner party and ask them about their dietary needs or preferences. We are engaging in hospitable curiosity when we ask people about the things in our spaces or institutions that make them feel welcome or unwelcome.

Lurid curiosity is a natural human temptation to know things for the sake of knowing them. It's the reason we all slow down when we're driving on the highway and there's evidence of a collision on the side of the road. We all want to know what happened even if we have no intention or ability to help. We just want to know. Entire traffic jams are caused so frequently by this need to know that we have a term for it, *a gawker delay*. In fact, sometimes gawkers even cause additional collisions when their efforts to see the details of a crash distract them from the road.

That's kind of what lurid curiosity does. It distracts us from what matters and harms people in the process. Lurid curiosity all too often treats others like exotic oddities, and it doesn't serve anyone but the curious. It is never hospitable to ask about the details of someone else's body or what they do with them in intimate relationships. This is what so often happens to transgender people. "But do they still have a penis?" "Are they going to have *the* surgery?" "Who are they going to date? How will that even work?" "Are they taking medication?" Lurid curiosity reduces transgender and nonbinary people to body parts. Teaching communities and individuals to identify the difference between hospitable and lurid curiosity empowers them to show up more faithfully in conversations around the trans community and inclusion.

But this body part thing is going to keep coming up. We are overwhelmingly obsessed, as a culture, with transgender people's bodies and their body parts. Quite frankly, it's gross. Whether it's about bathrooms, locker rooms, sports teams, or medical care, we hear the reductive reasoning that if they have a penis, they're a boy and if they don't, they're a girl. Furthermore, the concern from those who believe transgender children don't belong in spaces that align with their gender identity focuses on the danger of particular bodies and body parts. This is especially true for the outcry about transgender girls in girls' spaces. Transgender young people of color experience even greater scrutiny and denigration. If anyone is seeing someone's genitals in a bathroom, locker room, or a cabin at summer camp, we have a much bigger problem on our hands than what those genitals happen to be.

Practically speaking, normalizing privacy for young people benefits them all. It doesn't just help those who are transgender or gender expansive; it helps young people struggling with body image, living with eating disorders, and who have experienced sexual assault. It helps all young people to teach them they have a right to bodily autonomy including who sees their body, when, and on what terms. So whether it's a school locker room or a bathroom, the concern shouldn't be that there is someone with a penis in that space but instead that every person in that space deserves the right to privacy. Finally, the rhetoric around the very presence of a penis making a space inherently unsafe for girls points to something ugly about the way our culture treats boys. What message does that send to the cisgender boys we're raising? Vilifying bodies or body parts of any kind is dangerous and dehumanizing.

## UNSAFE VERSUS UNCOMFORTABLE

Remember, we want to put the transgender child at the center of what we do, protecting them with layers of support. But when we talk about protecting one child, inevitably people will ask why we're putting one child's needs over another. We hear this around these so-called bathroom debates all the time. If protecting a transgender child puts another child at risk, is it right? Well, a cisgender child is not actually at risk in the same way as a transgender child. We must differentiate between what it means to be uncomfortable and what it means to be unsafe.

If we're still talking about bathrooms, we know that gender-diverse people have an increased risk for assault in bathrooms when they are restricted from using facilities that align with their identity.[2] We also know that the emotional and mental impact of feeling unsafe in sex- or gender-segregated facilities increases their experiences of stigma and anxiety.[3] There is no data to support the idea that someone using the restroom with a gender-diverse person is actually unsafe.[4] Instead, they may be uncomfortable. We can support them in their discomfort, talking through their concerns and brainstorming possible alternatives for them, while protecting the safety of the gender-diverse person.

If we shift the conversation from bathrooms to churches, we know that when transgender and gender-diverse people are exposed to the words and ideas of those who say who they are isn't okay in the eyes of the God who created them, they are unsafe. Their emotional and mental well-being is impacted in a way that increases the risk for suicide, self-harm, and other risk-taking behaviors. People who believe transgender people aren't intended by God to be themselves are not made unsafe when we say otherwise. They are uncomfortable.

The clear differentiation between unsafe and uncomfortable allows us to show up in love and grace for people who disagree while caring for the children among us with the focus on protecting the most vulnerable child of God in our midst. This goes for every community our children are a part of, including their congregations. The priority is not to protect the budget or the attendance numbers. It's not to protect people's opinions of the church. In every area of our children's lives, we can help people differentiate between who is unsafe and who is uncomfortable and then consider how we best meet the different needs of each group. Most importantly, we do not allow people to be made unsafe in an effort to make others more comfortable. We are called as people of faith to love God and love each other. Love is hard. Acting in love in the face of fear is even harder. There will be bumps and challenges. There will certainly be conflict. But I can tell you that when we act in love, beautiful and holy things happen.

# 8 | CASEROLES AND MENTAL HEALTH

While I touched on Rebekah's experience with depression and anxiety when we talked about grief, it warrants a deeper dive. Our culture and our church are notoriously bad at caring for people in day-to-day mental health struggles and in mental health crisis. Nothing in any parenting book could have prepared me for a seven-year-old child who wanted to die. In the nine months prior to her social transition, Rebekah struggled. She went through an intense period of depression, and her previously mild anxiety escalated to debilitating.

At seven years old, she was a danger to herself and others. I don't know what to do with that, even having lived through it and come out the other side. Seven-year-olds are just so little. Her pain and struggle were so deep. I have never been so scared. We lived in crisis mode; all joy was gone. Our only goal on any given day was keeping us all safe. Through counseling, nutritional therapy, a wonderfully supportive doctor, and a deep trust in our kid, we were able to peel back the layers until we were left with the core issue of her identity, an issue she didn't even realize was at the core until we sat there together staring at it.

Caring for a loved one with mental illness or struggling with mental health is lonely. People don't usually understand what your loved one is going through, and they have no idea how they can help. Unfortunately, when people don't know what to do, it makes them uncomfortable, and as a culture, we tend to avoid things that are uncomfortable. In my hardest moments, I reached out to friends with a text or a call. At first, they'd respond, usually saying some things that weren't very helpful but they were trying nonetheless. When we were in a crisis, they'd suggest we call the police, but the police are not a safe option for someone in a mental health crisis, let alone when that person is seven years old. Many places in our country don't have any resources in place for those situations, or if they do, too many people don't know about them.

Other times, I'd confide in a friend how scared and sad I felt, how exhausted we were. Then, they might suggest I just needed to medicate my child while not understanding their medical care or our situation. Medication can be a really important tool in supporting mental health, but it doesn't magically make everything better, and it's not right for everyone. We underestimate the power of our presence when people are in pain. We think people need us to solve their problems when people just need us to love them, to sit with them when it's impossibly hard, to bear witness to their very real struggle. I wish my friends had the tools necessary to say, "I see you. I don't know what to do either, but I'm here with you in it." Eventually, I'd send a text, days or weeks later, and I'd simply get no response. They didn't know what to do, and they'd given up. That still hurts. I vividly remember sitting in the rocking chair in my bedroom, nursing my infant and sobbing. I was so scared. Our family was all alone in this.

## THE BLAME GAME

When I used to explain that my young child struggled with anxiety and depression, people were shocked and skeptical. What did she have to be stressed about? This is a radical misunderstanding of mental health and mental illness. Too often, we blame those struggling with mental illness for their symptoms, and when they are young people, we blame their parents. We are bombarded with messages about today's youth and their laziness, irresponsibility, and self-centeredness. Struggling young people are labeled manipulative and defiant or dismissed as looking for attention. Their parents are cast as indulgent, weak, or negligent. Maybe they just didn't pray hard enough. These labels become barriers to communities shouldering up to families and young people when they need it the most.

While, as we've already seen, support and affirmation of gender-diverse young people drastically reduce their risk of suicide and the rates of anxiety and depression, mental health continues to be a critical conversation for these young people, as it is with all young people. Marginalized communities are especially at risk for ongoing mental health struggles. Let me reiterate that these young people do not struggle because there is something wrong with them but because of the rejection, harassment, discrimination, and uncertainty they face in society. Even a child with the most loving home must go out into a world that simply isn't safe.

Some symptoms of depression and anxiety are a result of the oppression marginalized people experience in the world. Transgender and nonbinary youth who experience oppression in relation to two or more of their identities are increasingly at risk. There are also people who live with clinically diagnosed mental illness and happen to be transgender or nonbinary. For many people, it could be a combination of both. Outside of a clinical care setting, I'm not sure that it's necessary to pull apart those two threads. Instead, let's focus on ensuring all transgender and nonbinary people and all people living with symptoms of mental health struggles or mental illness know they are worthy of love, support, and medical attention. Their struggles are not a result of a failure on their part. And we must work to dismantle the systems of oppression that cause or exacerbate marginalized communities' experiences of mental illness and act as barriers to systems of care.

Given that this book is rooted in a Christian faith perspective, it would be irresponsible of me to not name the ways the church has contributed to stigma and lack of understanding for people experiencing mental illness. In her book *All Who Are Weary*, Emmy Kegler writes about how the church historically saw mental illness as a result of sin or maybe a test of faith. These ideas suggest that if people just believed better, trusted the Bible more, and acted in more godly ways, they would be cured of what ails them. Just pray harder, and you will be fine. This intersects with the ways the church has treated LGBTQ+ people, encouraging them to pray away their identities, compounding the impact of this kind of spiritual bypassing and reckless theology on queer people, including gender-diverse young people. Kegler writes, "What if the church taught that toxic positivity and denying medical attention to those in distress was a sin?"[1] We can also teach that it is a sin to tell transgender and nonbinary people that who they are somehow goes against God's plan. That is a powerful place to start.

## DESTIGMATIZE AND NORMALIZE

To show up for the young people in our lives, and anyone struggling with depression, anxiety, or any other mental illness, we have to destigmatize the conversation and the experience. The conversation around health has shifted some since the COVID-19 pandemic. I think more people are aware of mental health needs because more people were and are struggling, but still too often the conversation is shrouded in shame. People experience mental health struggles and illness for all sorts of reasons including trauma, genetics, chronic illness, nutritional imbalances, and more. The vast majority of transgender and nonbinary youth are impacted at some point by depression and anxiety. In the world in which we live, it could arguably be considered unhealthy to not be impacted. We are still reeling from a global pandemic. We're experiencing a climate crisis. There are wars and ongoing global security threats. We're on the verge of a global financial crisis. And the political landscape has become increasingly fraught with real implications for our daily lives and personal rights. If you're not overwhelmed, you're likely not paying attention. Normalizing our feelings and mental health experiences is critical to being able to have conversations that aren't mired in shame. It is okay to not be okay.

## FIND RESOURCES

Resources are tricky, but they're out there. Following the pandemic, mental health services were increasingly hard to find as our system bowed under the weight of increased demand. Finding mental health services you can afford is another layer of difficulty. In moments or periods of crisis, there are some national numbers you can call. Sometimes they can connect you to or recommend more local support, but at the very least, they can hopefully get you through that moment. If you dial 988, you'll get the suicide and crisis lifeline. The Trevor Project hosts an LGBTQ-specific hotline that can be reached via web, text, or phone. Trans LifeLine (877-565-8860) is a transgender-specific crisis number. The National Alliance on Mental Illness (NAMI) is a national organization with local chapters as well as a helpline and extensive web resources. Finally, PFLAG is another national organization I mentioned earlier with local chapters supporting parents and family members of LGBTQ+ people. They are often connected to local mental health providers and resources.

## SHOW UP

Church members are almost always willing to show up with a casserole or a dozen of them when a family member is ill or injured, be it a cancer diagnosis or a knee surgery. Unfortunately, families struggling with mental illness are often abandoned. We can do better. Instead of asking how we can help, offer a specific kind of help. *Can I bring you a meal? Would you like me to babysit so you can take a break? I'm running to the store; can I pick you something up?* Additionally, normalizing the conversation around mental health makes it easier for families to ask for help or speak up when they're struggling. Perhaps most importantly, don't assume everyone is okay. So many of us use everything we can to get through the public-facing parts of our day and then fall apart when we get home.

If we're going to talk about mental health struggles in transgender and nonbinary young people, we must also cover the mental and emotional toll that raising a gender-diverse child takes on caregivers. Parents and young people experience extreme levels of stress and trauma related to the landscape around transgender and nonbinary people in the world right now. Raising gender-diverse children in faith requires communities to rally around their parents as they work tirelessly to build a world where all children can be safe, loved, and successful.

There is very real trauma involved in raising these young people, especially if you're in a state where laws are being enacted that harm children like yours. Many families are actively trying to flee states where they aren't safe. Others are doing their best to care for themselves and their children while living under constant attack. The worst bullying our families experience often comes from adults, whether neighbors or elected officials, and that is its own source of trauma. Families, of course, may also experience trauma unrelated to raising a transgender young person, including that caused by systems of oppression, ruptured relationships, economic instability, and food or housing insecurity, which in turn creates more complex layers of struggle. Create spaces where parents and caregivers can connect with one another. If you're a parent, find someone you can talk to—your friends, family, or a counselor. You cannot do this alone. Prioritize whatever you can that helps you fill yourself up when so much is depleting you. Ask for help when you can. There is not a singular right way to navigate this, and I am certain you are doing the very best you can. Your kid knows that too.

## LOVE AND GRACE

Love and grace are the two single most important ideas for my faith and my understanding of the world and my role in it, so much so that I have the words tattooed on my wrist. My tattoo reads "love; grace." Love and grace remind me of everything I know to be true about God. God's expansive love is bigger than anything I can imagine, and it's for me. God loves me more than I can comprehend, and that love compels me to love others with abandon. I do my best to lead with love—in my home, in my advocacy, and in the world. But I'm human, and I mess up all the time. That's where grace comes in. I can be absurdly hard on myself. I constantly feel like I'm not doing enough or that I'm simply not enough. God's grace reminds me that I am always enough. I can't do anything to earn or jeopardize God's love for me, and that is something I carry into the world as I encounter other human beings who are equally flawed. God's grace is for them too. God's scandalous grace might frustrate me when I'm reminded that even those who are making my life hardest right now are equal recipients, but that same scandalous grace also reminds me that we are indeed all God's creation and members of the body of Christ. I'm a better human to myself, the people I love, and everyone else I encounter when I'm grounded in love and grace.

And then there's that semicolon. The semicolon is inspired by Project Semicolon, a nonprofit dedicated to suicide prevention and awareness. The semicolon means that this isn't the end of your story. There's no period here. There's more to live; there's more to learn. I got this tattooed on my wrist because of my own struggles with depression and anxiety. It's a commitment to myself and to the people I care about that those things won't be the end of my story. I share that here because many people have tried to discredit me as an advocate and as a mother because of my history with depression and anxiety. I refuse to let them win or let them shame me into silence.

Experiencing mental illness doesn't make you an unfit parent or a flawed human any more than the fact that we are all imperfect. I also share it because the experience of raising a transgender child has challenged me in more ways than one, including my own mental health. I have had to be honest with my family and loved ones about my bandwidth to cope, at any given time, with the things that are thrown at us. Sometimes it means taking a break from advocacy for periods of time; other times it means taking a break from adulting. It means knowing that when news of attacks on families like ours comes out, I need to carve out space first to care for my child and then to care for myself.

I can't just keep going like the world isn't on fire because it is on fire, in so many ways. None of this is normal or okay. It's not okay for families to have to fight to have access to evidence-based medical care their children require because of politicians. It's not okay for families to have to put together safe folders of documentation to help protect them when Child Protective Services show up at their door because they're being used as political pawns. It's not okay for me to worry if the parents on the sidelines at my kid's field hockey game are going to decide that today is the day they're not okay having a transgender player on the team.

When you live your life holding your breath, waiting for it all to blow up in your face, you're not going to feel okay all the time. So if it doesn't feel normal or okay, that's legitimate. As we're living in these times of so much not okayness, do whatever you need to care for yourselves and your people. I've been learning better how to do this from the Black women in my life who have been protecting their families and fighting for justice for decades. We will keep fighting. We will keep telling the world how not okay it is. And we will keep showing up to take care of each other because we belong to one another as families raising vulnerable kids, as siblings in Christ, and as human beings on this planet at this time. Let me say it one more time: it's okay to not be okay because none of this is okay.

# 9 | WHO GOD MADE ME TO BE

At the Children's Hospital of Philadelphia, we work with a world-class team of medical professionals for all of Rebekah's gender-related health care. When we first met with Dr. Hawkins, a psychotherapist and codirector at the clinic, Rebekah was eight years old. First, Dr. Hawkins spoke with me and my husband, and then she left to talk with Rebekah. When Dr. Hawkins returned to the office where we were waiting, she had tears in her eyes. While getting to know Rebekah, she asked Rebekah how she would respond to someone who didn't understand what it means to be transgender. Rebekah's honest answer was simple and clear: "Being transgender means being who God created me to be."

This is at the root of how we approach raising transgender, nonbinary, and gender-nonconforming children in faith. This is who God created them to be. You do not have to choose between your child and your faith. The truth is you may have to choose between your child and your church, but we'll get to that later. First, I need you to know deep in your soul that gender-diverse people of all ages are whole and holy. They are made in God's own image, and they are exactly who God created them to be. After all, God does not make mistakes.

## IMAGO DEI

Christians believe that humans are created in God's image. This belief is first established in Genesis 1:26, "Then God said, 'Let us make humankind in our image, according to our likeness,'" and is referred to as *imago Dei*, the image of God. A deep connection between God and humanity separates us from the rest of God's creations. In a world dominated by Greek philosophy, the *imago Dei* was seen most deeply in humans' ability to engage in moral, spiritual, or intellectual thought. Some examples would be rational thinking, creative freedom, a possibility for self-actualization, and the ability for self-transcendence.

Later scholars would suggest that *imago Dei* was related to our concrete physicality, a bodily connection between us and the divine, while others believed it related to our place in the world and how we related to God's creation.[1] Whether it is our ability for rational or creative thought, or the beautiful diversity of the physical bodies we inhabit, or in the way we build relationships and communities that extend beyond ourselves, the idea of *imago Dei*, the image of God being recognized in both the divine and in humankind, links us to each other. It is the common denominator that connects all of humanity. Since we are all made in God's image, then the image of God is something that we should be able to see in one another.

Sometimes that idea is diluted down to a Sunday school lesson of how we are to treat one another. While I do believe the sentiment that we're all made in God's image is a powerful indicator for how we are called to be in community together, *imago Dei* points to something beyond a "do unto others" message. All humans, including gender-expansive, transgender, and nonbinary humans, were created in God's own image. That means that God must be all those things too. If we know transgender and gender- diverse humans exist (and we know they do throughout history and around the world) and that they were made in God's own image, then we know that God's image is gender diverse. That means something really cool for our own understanding of God and our faith. If God is gender diverse, there are parts of God we are missing out on if there are not gender-diverse people in our midst. Transgender and gender-expansive people teach us more about the God who created all of us and give us a fuller understanding of our faith. They are a gift to the church and the world. It also means we're not called to care for our transgender and gender-expansive siblings as some sort of service to those less fortunate. This is not charity. Instead, we know that transgender and gender-expansive people allow us to see and know parts of God we wouldn't otherwise see or know.

## SUNRISE, SUNSET

If we go one verse further to Genesis 1:27, we read, "So God created humans in his image, in the image of God he created them; male and female he created them." Of course, it's probably more accurate to remove the masculine language the New Revised Standard Version (NRSV) uses for God. God isn't actually male; God is so much more. Instead, the text could read something like this: "So God created humans in [God's] image, in the image of God, [God] created them; male and female [God] created them."

First, let me say that gendered language in the Bible is a struggle for translators, whether the text is referring to God or groups of people. They must make educated guesses about what the original text intended based on the context, the culture of the day, and the presumed audience. Their own conscious or unconscious biases play a part too. Centuries of patriarchal Christian societies assumed God's default gender was male based on their worldview while reinforcing that same worldview by continually describing the Divine with male vocabulary. Resources like *The Inclusive Bible: The First Egalitarian Translation* can help us when gendered language limits access to the meaning of a particular text. Joe Dearborn, an editor of *The Inclusive Bible*, says part of their work was to "determine whether it is the linguistic convention used that expresses a sexist bias or whether the text itself is sexist in its meaning"[2] with the hope of getting as close to what the original text was trying to convey. In *The Inclusive Bible* translation, Genesis 1:27 reads, "Humankind was created as God's reflection: in the divine image God created them; female and male, God made them."

Regardless of translation, this is a verse that is frequently used to argue that the gender binary is biblically intentional. We were created to check the box that God checked for us, and that is that. But this feels like a limiting way to see the world, especially when we consider the rest of what God created. Theologians like Rev. Asher O'Callaghan, Austen Hartke, and Rev. M. Jade Kaiser have helped me better understand the biblical language used here and connect what I know to be true about God's beautiful creation to the beauty of diversity in bodies and gender.

Austen Hartke describes in his book *Transforming: The Bible and the Lives of Transgender Christians* how the work of making order from chaos, organizing, and categorizing would have been understood and important to Hebrew people in the ancient world.[3] Clear rules like "eat this, not that" kept them safe and helped them understand the world around them. In a conversation with Hartke, Rev. M. Jade Keiser points out that just because we have dichotomies of day and night, land and water, it doesn't mean we don't have dusk or marshes. These binaries aren't meant to say we have this, that, and absolutely nothing else.

As someone who has always most deeply connected to God and my faith in nature, this not only resonated but gave me language to better articulate my experience as a parent of a transgender child. My child is not lacking because she doesn't fit into what others perceive as the limits (or limitations) of "male and female"; she is no more "less than" or "broken" than we'd consider a sunset or a sunrise when we talk about day and night. Who hasn't looked at the sky at dawn and wondered at God's incredible creation? For me, the in-between places at the edge of the water and land are particularly special. They are sacred to me. Ocean waves crashing onto the beach, tiptoeing through a mountain stream, or tromping after my younger children on adventures through the marshland behind our home all involve places where I have felt especially close to God. These are holy places, in between and apart from, simultaneously both and neither. That's my experience of raising a transgender child and of knowing the most wonderful gender-diverse humans.

Rev. Asher O'Callaghan expressed this so beautifully:

In the beginning God created day and night. But have you ever seen a sunset!?!? Well trans and non-binary people are kind of like that. Gorgeous. Full of a hundred shades of color you can't see in plain daylight or during the night.

In the beginning God created land and sea. But have you ever seen a beach?!?! Well trans and non-binary people are kind of like that. Beautiful. A balanced oasis that's not quite like the ocean, nor quite like the land.

In the beginning God created birds of the air and fish of the sea. But have you ever seen a flying fish, or a duck or a puffin that swims and flies, spending lots of time in the water and on the land!?!? Well trans and non-binary people are kind of like that. Full of life. A creative combination of characteristics that blows people's minds.

In the beginning God also created male and female, in God's own image, God created them. So in the same way that God created realities in between, outside of, and beyond night and day, land and sea, or fish and birds, so God also created people with genders beyond male and female. Trans and non-binary and agender and intersex, God created us. All different sorts of people for all different sorts of relationships. Created from love to love and be loved. In God's image we live.[4]

## BODY OF CHRIST

I've loved the description of the body of Christ in 1 Corinthians 12 since I first heard the text in youth group as a middle schooler. We did an activity where we all had to be different parts of the body and work together. I don't remember the details, but the text stayed close to my heart all these years.

The body of Christ is made up of many parts, all with different gifts and roles: "If the foot would say, 'Because I am not a hand, I do not belong to the body,' that would not make it any less a part of the body" (1 Cor. 12:15). Just because we are different, it doesn't make us any less parts of the body: "If the whole body were an eye, where would the hearing be? If the whole body were hearing, where would the sense of smell be?" (1 Cor. 12:17) We need each other. We're missing things without the many and various parts of the body. The text goes on to say that the members of the body that seem to be weaker are indispensable. And then it talks about how.

> But God has so arranged the body, giving the greater honor to the inferior member, that there may be no dissension within the body, but the members may have the same care for one another. If one member suffers, all suffer together with it; if one member is honored, all rejoice together with it. (1 Cor. 12:24–26)

This text reminds us how deeply connected we are to one another. We can't simply say, "You aren't what I thought my sibling in Christ would be like. I don't need you." We need every single part. In fact, we honor those who are considered inferior so there is no dissension. How can anyone read this text and not see a biblical call to inclusion and justice? Some of us unjustly have privilege in our society because of who we are, the color of our skin, the families we come from, or the bodies we're born into. That's not God's design, but that's as true of society today as it was in biblical times. It's our job to care for and clothe with honor those parts that aren't as privileged. If one of us is suffering, we're all suffering. This calls us to community, inclusion, and advocacy, which we'll talk more about later.

The body of Christ is not fully present without our transgender and gender-expansive siblings. When we intentionally or unintentionally exclude part of the body of Christ, it suffers. The Bible is clear that when one part suffers, we all suffer. Gender-diverse people are a part of God's creation and a part of the body of Christ in the world. We are part of the same body. That unifies us. No matter what we do, we are in this together as members of the body of Christ. No matter how different we are, we share this identity. But our individual experiences are not erased by that unity. We remain uniquely gifted, uniquely called, and have unique experiences of harm and prosperity in the world.

This unique togetherness lays the groundwork for inclusion and celebration in faith settings. In fact, it once again moves our understanding from thinking that we need to welcome those gender-diverse children for their sake to understanding that we need them in our communities for our sake and for the sake of the gospel. Remember, being gender inclusive benefits everyone. We are not saviors. We are not helping the poor transgender humans. We are opening ourselves to understand God better and make more real and more present the kingdom of God here on earth.

## GENDER-BENDERS OF THE BIBLE

Those who suggest being transgender isn't biblical point to a few places in Scripture as evidence. There is generally more to the story of these verses than opponents suggest (just as we saw in Gen. 1:27), but perhaps of even greater significance, there are examples of important characters in Scripture who live outside of the gender norms of their day in one way or another. It can be a powerful shift to stop arguing the negative, stop digging into the same few verses opponents demand we consider, and look at the other stories the Bible tells. These characters who transgress gender expectations or limitations are helpful for us today as we look to raise transgender and nonbinary young people in faith. All of God's children deserve to know there has always been a place in God's kingdom for those who find themselves outside of the gender binary.

First, let's look at the "traditional" matriarchs in Scripture, who, rather than sitting meekly and quietly, laughed, fought, tricked, and lied as a part of the story of how God's people came to be in the world. Whether we are talking about Miriam, Deborah, Rebekah, or Rahab in the Hebrew Bible or any of the multiple Marys who stand alongside Jesus in the New Testament, these women pushed aside traditional gender roles as part of God's work in the world. Like Esther, each of them was called for "such a time as this" (Esther 4:14). They were not brought forth in spite of their unwillingness to adhere to gender expectations; instead, their willingness to step outside of those expectations is what drives God's story forward.

Next, consider the place of the eunuch within Scripture. Eunuchs were men who had been castrated, having their testicles crushed or removed. Often this happened in war, either as a punishment or to end a royal lineage. We cannot easily make direct comparisons from the experience of eunuchs to the experience of transgender people today. They lived in a different context, time, and place, and they were often made eunuchs against their will. However, eunuchs in biblical times do give us examples of people who lived outside the gender norms of the time and how the Bible speaks of them in contrast to how society speaks of them.

The story of Philip and the Ethiopian eunuch from Acts chapter 8 is popular in Bible studies and stands out in LGBTQ+

communities. An angel appears to the disciple Philip (also known as Philip the Evangelist) and says, "You should go down this road in the wilderness." Being a good disciple with plenty of time on his hands Philip does just that without asking any questions. While on the road, Philip meets someone. The text says this person is Ethiopian, a eunuch, and a court official in charge of the queen's treasury. Those are a lot of details for someone who remains nameless; these details must be important. The Ethiopian stranger is reading the scroll of Isaiah while traveling home in his chariot, and the Spirit tells Philip, "Go join the chariot." When Philip gets there, he hears the chariot rider reading Isaiah and asks, "Do you understand what you're reading?" The Ethiopian traveler says, "How can I without a guide?" and invites Philip for a ride. Philip interprets a specific section of Isaiah, connecting it to Jesus, and then proceeds to share the gospel story. The Ethiopian, seeing some water along the road, responds to what he's hearing by saying, "Look, here is water! What is to prevent me from being baptized?" We never hear a reply from Philip, but the text says they go down to the water. Philip baptizes our Ethiopian friend and is then promptly snatched away by the Holy Spirit never to be seen again by our joy-filled new sibling in Christ.

This story features someone, an outsider in every way, who, based on everything we know, should not have been welcomed; they aren't like any of the other characters in the New Testament so far. The Ethiopian eunuch was a stranger who didn't look like any of those early disciples, who as a eunuch was physically outside of bodily norms and was either an enslaved person or formerly enslaved to a foreign queen. They already knew something of Judaism, but for all the reasons already stated, they wouldn't have been allowed too far into the temple complex, if they even made it in the front gate. And yet after they heard the story of Jesus, they fortuitously found water by the road and asked, "What is to prevent me from being baptized?" This outsider was then baptized by one of the original twelve disciples. There were no further questions or requirements. It just happened. The font was wide open for this child of God, who no one would have expected to be included.

The story of the Ethiopian eunuch is just one of many times eunuchs appear in Scripture. We read more about the way eunuchs are part of God's story in Isaiah 56. This passage can again show us how God would turn the tables on society's expectations and cultural norms. Isaiah writes,

Do not let the eunuch say,
"I am just a dry tree."
For thus says the LORD:
To the eunuchs who keep my sabbaths,
who choose the things that please me
and hold fast my covenant,
I will give, in my house and within my walls,
a monument and a name
better than sons and daughters;
I will give them an everlasting name
that shall not be cut off.

In his book, Austen Hartke cites this passage as being particularly important for him. Placing it within Israel's exilic return from Babylon, he says that into a historical context when the Israelites were trying to rebuild a country from ruins, "God spoke an unprecedented word of inclusion."[5] While their stories may be different, we can certainly draw a number of connections between the eunuch of the ancient world and the transgender person of today—marginalization, ridicule, and the injustice of having laws written about you without having any say in those laws. God not only welcomes the eunuch of Isaiah's time; God promised them a place and a name and a community.

In Genesis 37, we find yet another example of gender non-conformity in the Bible. It's a story many believe they know, but it's far more colorful than even they realize. This is the story of Joseph and his coat of many colors (even if that's not a very good translation—but more on that in a bit). Joseph is the twelfth of thirteen children, and at seventeen years old, he spends his time helping his father's wives. He has a couple of dreams that seem to indicate the rest of his family will bow down to him, and his brothers get rather upset. They get so upset that they beat him up, fake his death, and sell him into slavery in Egypt. Eventually, Joseph ends up in a position of great power and saves his family from a regionwide famine. Joseph's story sets the stage for the book of Exodus and the continuing story of God and God's chosen people.

Much has been said about the ambiguous Hebrew word used to describe Joseph's coat. The term only shows up in one other place in the Bible (2 Sam 13:18–19) in reference to an extravagant robe worn by Tamar, the virgin princess of King David. We just don't know if the words used in Genesis and 1 Samuel refer to the extravagance of the gift or the gender of the person who traditionally wore the robe. Either way, after an already tumultuous relationship with his brothers, Joseph's father giving him this robe is the final piece that sets him apart from his brothers. There's so much more to the story though.

In his book *In the Margins: A Transgender Man's Journey with Scripture*, Father Shannon T. L. Kearns explains that Joseph was the youngest son of Jacob, himself described in less masculine terms than his brother Esau. Kearns writes, "One wonders if Jacob saw something of himself in Joseph. In the way Joseph moved and talked. In the way he preferred the company of women. In the way he carried himself."[6] When we read the Joseph story through a lens of gender-based trauma, it is easy to see that Joseph didn't conform to the roles and expectations that his brothers set for him. From his work with Jacob's wives instead of being out in the fields to his ability to interpret dreams, he finds himself in a place outside and apart, even while he is loved and cherished by his father. Kearns describes how Joseph's brothers ripped up that coat of many colors, the physical representation of their discomfort and frustration at their brother's nonconformity. Despite his brothers' betrayal and the hardships he would endure, the final arc of the Joseph story reunites him with his family and puts him in a place where he can both provide for the physical needs and forgive them for the actions of their past. Once again, goodness and favor prevail for those who live on the edge of what is expected of them, who don't, or even can't, conform.

## EQUITY AND TRUTH

Many transgender and gender-diverse people take heart and comfort in Galatians 3:28, where we are reminded that in Jesus, "there is no longer Jew or Greek; there is no longer slave or free; there is no longer male and female, for all of you are one in Christ Jesus." It's not that our genders are erased, but we are reminded we are one in Christ, just as we saw in 1 Corinthians 12. We are all part of one body, and there is no longer inequity or difference in status between Jew or Greek, slave or free, male or female. It's important to recognize that this verse has been used to harm the Jewish community and contribute to Jewish erasure. That was not its original intent. It was a word of grace spoken to Gentiles, assuring them that conversion to Judaism wasn't required to be a disciple of Jesus.

The verse speaks a similar word of grace to transgender and gender-diverse people today who see it is as a reminder that regardless of who we are or where we come from, we are all equally worthy of God's love and goodness. Knowing that it doesn't erase those identities but addresses the inequalities therein, I might be so bold as to think that if it were written today, it might also say there is no longer "cisgender or transgender, straight or queer." I would no more want to erase transgender and queer identities than I would Jewish ones but instead erase the division and judgment between them. That being said, we need to proceed with care and clarity when discussing this verse, always denouncing anti-Semitism and Jewish erasure.

Finally, I always come back to Jeremiah 1:15, "Before I formed you in the womb I knew you, and before you were born I consecrated you; I appointed you a prophet to the nations." God called Jeremiah at a very young age to speak truth to power, but Jeremiah was scared and hesitant. Jeremiah was arguing with God that he was too young and not ready for the work ahead, but God basically said, "I know you're young; I created you, I know everything about you, and I have a purpose for you." Even when the journey ahead feels too hard, too daunting, we can remember that just like Jeremiah, God created each of us and has a purpose for us all. We believe in a God who knows us intimately, loves us unconditionally, and calls us to the work of truth and justice. When that work is challenging, when it feels like the way we are called to love and advocate for one other is too disruptive, may you find comfort and courage in knowing that God created both you and the gender-expansive people you love. God has known each of you to be who you are from the beginning, even when other people may not have. God knows each of you in the wholeness of your being—body, mind, and spirit. And what we know from Genesis is that God's creation is, indeed, good.

## THAT'S A GOD THING

That was just a taste of the complex exegetical conversation around gender diversity in the Bible. But I believe our faith has a much simpler answer for our children. I may get in trouble for saying this. I know I'm supposed to defer to deep theological reasoning and complicated biblical exegesis. But if I've learned anything from my two degrees in religion, it's that complicated isn't always better and that God things aren't always best explained in theological terms. Sometimes it's as simple as Rebekah knowing that being transgender is being who God made her to be. God doesn't want God's children to live in pain. God didn't create them to be broken. But when gender-diverse people can't be their fullest selves, pain and brokenness are precisely what happens. When Rebekah was pretending to be someone she wasn't, she was hurting. She was hurting so badly she wanted to die. At seven years old, she wanted to die. That was not God's plan for her. I don't need an advanced degree in religion or a "reverend" title to know that. When she stepped into her identity, her joy and confidence exploded. Her ability to spread kindness and do good increased exponentially. That's a God thing.

God speaks to us in a myriad of ways. God shows up in our lives at unexpected times in unexpected people. Our God is not a god of neat and tidy by-the-book rules but a god who turns things on their head, defies expectation, and scandalizes us with their grace and love. Let's stop looking for God only in the pages of a book or in the walls of a church building. Let's be willing to see God staring back at us through the eyes of a child who is finally sharing their truest selves with us and the world.

Without access to complex biblical interpretation theological education, parents have been discovering this God thing for a long time. The hardest part is that all too often, they struggled deeply first and harmed their kids in the process before finally deciding to choose their child over what their church was teaching or what they believed their church was teaching. And yet, so many times, parents have gotten there anyway. Against the odds, parents of many generations have journeyed from thinking their child was wrong to seeing that their child is exactly who God made them to be. And that goes for grown-up children too. Still others never quite find their way. Any harm in the name of faith is too much harm. So what can we do to avoid that? Well, that's what we're tackling next.

I said at the beginning of this chapter that families must know they don't have to choose between their children and their faith. But unfortunately, sometimes families need to choose between their children and their church. If your church cannot fully and unapologetically love, affirm, and celebrate your child's truest self without any caveats, then your church is a harmful place for that child. Kevin Miguel Garcia, a pastor and advocate, wrote in their book *Bad Theology Kills* about their own experience in the church and at the hands of harmful theology. They made it out alive, but they know all too well others didn't and won't. It's not an exaggeration to say bad theology kills. It does. Believing that who you are at your core is somehow at odds with the God who created you, that the God you worship believes who you are isn't okay or worthy of love, that who you are is a sin for which you must repent is irreparably damaging.

People exposed to this type of theology may leave their faith and never return, may live with the religious trauma they've experienced forever, or may lose themselves to drugs, alcohol, or suicide. Remember, the data tells us that when it comes to suicidality, faith generally has a protective factor. That means that usually young people with connections to faith communities are at a decreased risk for suicide. But we see the opposite when we look at LGBTQ+ young people, faith, and suicide. LGBTQ+ young people whose faith is important to them struggle more deeply and are at a higher risk for suicide. Bad theology kills. Please don't expose your children to that any longer than you already have. Tell them the church was wrong and walk away. You cannot stay in a congregation that teaches that being transgender is a sin, that being LGBTQ+ is a sin, and love your child well. Your continuing to commit time, energy, and, probably, dollars to that community speaks volumes to that child even if they are grown and living on their own. Those churches, that theology, and the politics associated with them continue to do unspeakable harm to this community.

The next chapter will dig into ways that churches can do better and show up for our gender-diverse children, but if your church can't do these things, then it's time to walk away and find another one. God isn't the problem here, but the institution that claims to know God and speak for God in a way that does harm most certainly is a problem. Honestly, if it came down to it, I would rather see families leave their faith behind altogether than stay in a toxic and harmful religious space. The good news is you don't need to leave your faith behind altogether, but it is important that you walk away from any space that is teaching that LGBTQ+ people are anything other than whole and holy.

# 10 | LOVE A LITTLE LOUDER

At seventeen years old, Tor was a church kid, through and through. Tor was raised in a Lutheran congregation. Their faith was important to them, and they loved their church community. Yet as they came to understand their identity and their sexuality, they had no idea if who they were was okay in the eyes of the church, in the eyes of God. Their congregation had never said anything particularly bad about LGBTQ+ people, but they'd never said anything good either. Tor, left to figure things out on their own, went to the internet to see what their faith said about LGBTQ+ identities. The harmful theology they found left them feeling scared and alone. This theology made them unsure of whether they could be themselves and still be loved by God. This young person experienced deep pain because their faith community politely refused to talk about LGBTQ+ people. The struggle that followed for Tor, their feelings of being bad and sinful, wasn't because their church was saying all of that. It was the result of their church not saying anything at all and leaving Tor to figure it out by themselves with Google as their guide.

Tor told their story at an event in New Jersey centered around creating safer and more welcoming churches for LGBTQ+ youth. Tor implored the community gathered to "love a little louder" so that young people like Tor wouldn't have to question whether or not they are beloved children of God. I'd actually say our churches need to love a lot louder. Imagine how Tor's story might have been different if their church had boldly, loudly, and joyfully proclaimed that LGBTQ+ people are fearfully and wonderfully made by a God who knows and loves them.

In this chapter, we'll look at the practical ways we create inclusive faith communities for gender-diverse young people both in what we do and what we don't do. Earlier, I explained that when Rebekah started public school, I brought them a detailed packet of information about supporting transgender and gender-diverse kids in schools. I told them I needed a meeting with the principal and that he would need to read that packet first. This chapter is that packet for families walking into a congregation ready to have a conversation with the pastor or leaders about how to support their child in faith. Honestly, it would serve the church and its families if faith leaders read the whole book, but this chapter is a good start. We talked a little bit about theology in the last chapter, but continuing to grow in your understanding of God's creation and celebration of transgender and gender-diverse people is a powerful step in your inclusion journey. Grounded in an ever-deepening understanding of the theology, let's look at accessible next steps in other areas of congregational life.

## REPRESENTATION

Representation matters. It's important for gender-diverse people to see themselves in the church around them. Perhaps even more importantly, those who are not gender diverse need to see gender-diverse people and their stories lifted up in our faith communities. In worship, this can be accomplished in sermon illustrations or by naming them in the prayers. Use a picture book with a gender-expansive character for a children's sermon. Include gender-diverse people of all ages, races, expressions, and abilities. Think outside the box and get creative. We all get to know God better when we know more of God's creation. *Transgender* isn't a dirty word. Let's stop acting like it is. It's appropriate for people of all ages to learn about the kinds of humans God created. Some of those humans are transgender.

If we go back to Tor's story, if they had simply heard people like themselves lifted up in the prayers of the church or portrayed in stories told during sermons, they would have had a fundamentally different understanding of what the church thought about them. The church felt that this was a topic they should stay out of or that it wasn't relevant to their community. Of course, Tor was a part of their community (and statistically, other gender-diverse people were undoubtedly present there too). Tor was left confused and having to figure things out on their own because they never heard LGBTQ+ people referenced. It's important to name, intentionally and specifically, transgender and gender-diverse people in the life of the church.

To continue to expand representation, diversify your bookshelves so they include a variety of voices and perspectives. Reading about people who are different from us helps us access empathy and increases our understanding of and appreciation for God's glorious creation. Make sure your entire community has access to and understands the importance of diverse literature. Are there resources in your church that talk about LGBTQ+-affirming theology? Check out the list in the back of the book for some suggestions.

RAISING KIDS BEYOND THE BINARY

What about representation in leadership in the church? Do you have transgender and gender-diverse staff? Congregational leaders? Does your constitution create space for that kind of leadership? Some constitutions require that congregational councils have a certain percentage of women members and a certain percentage of men. This was intended to increase representation of women in leadership, but what happens if you have a nonbinary person who would like to serve? Look at your policies. See what needs to change so there is space for everyone at the table.

## LANGUAGE

Language is always important but especially so in worship. Small shifts make a big difference in including more people. For instance, instead of saying "brothers and sisters in Christ," say "siblings" to include those who fall outside of the binary. Look at your prayers, liturgies, and hymns. Examine the way gendered language is used. You'll probably learn a lot! Then consider the language you use for God. As we look to make our language more gender inclusive, it benefits all people to stop assuming masculine language is appropriate or correct for God. It's simply been the norm for centuries. When asked, most of us would describe a God that is far beyond any gender, but we continue to allow masculine language to dominate the way we talk about the Divine. Simply refer to God as "God," or intentionally switch things up and use "they" or "she" to refer to God. We're not suggesting that God is exclusively feminine or inherently nonbinary (although that may be worth diving into a little deeper); we're simply compensating for centuries of prioritizing masculinity.

Pronouns also play a big role in our ability to welcome and include gender-diverse people. Normalizing sharing pronouns in church settings helps people communicate the language they'd like others to use when referring to them and encourages people to not assume how others identify. Add pronouns to name tags. Use them when you introduce yourself in groups. Add them to the website next to staff names. A caveat: Please don't ever require someone to share their pronouns. They may not be comfortable doing so for reasons that are all their own, but we can create an environment where pronouns are offered regularly to help the community make it a habit. I talk extensively about pronouns in prior chapters, so if you jumped in here for the church perspective, maybe that's a reason to start at the beginning.

We can also notice the ways we are using gendered language to refer to people. When we ask children to find their adult figure, do we tell them to find their mom or dad? Well, that excludes lots of families, including families with nonbinary parents but also children who live with guardians, grandparents, aunts, uncles, or beyond. My first full-time job was as the director of a children's fitness center that taught sports classes, gymnastics classes, and what were commonly known as "mommy and me" classes. The marketing material described them as "parent participation," but even that failed to encompass the many kinds of adults that attended classes with the toddler in their life. So we called the parents, grandparents, neighbors, nannies, and whoever else might attend class "grown-ups." "Grown-ups, don't forget to sign in!" "Alright, friends, bring your grown-up to the circle so we can play a game!" Simple and effective. I still say "your grown-up" when I'm talking to younger children, or if they're teenagers, "your trusted adult" or just "your adult." I worked with a major athletic brand that talked about "youth and their empowering adults." How beautiful! I want every young person to recognize their parents or guardians as empowering adults in their lives.

## POLICIES AND PRACTICES

When it comes to the administrative side of things, look at forms and policies. On new member forms, Sunday school registration, or anytime we collect data from people, what are we asking for and why? If we are asking for gender, is there a reason? Often, people collect gender data as a default. It's what we've always done; it's what everyone does. But do we actually need to know someone's gender to teach them in Christian education classes or to welcome them as a new member? Generally, we don't. I worked with the New Jersey Synod of the ELCA to develop policies around ministry with LGBTQ+ young people, and one policy we recommended was to *not* ask for gender unless it was specifically necessary due to the nature of the event.

For youth ministry, that meant asking for gender when we provided housing as that was determined by gender identity. For a virtual event or a single-day event without overnight accommodations, we simply stopped asking for gender information. It wasn't relevant. Additionally, when we did ask for gender, we always included a nonbinary option. That didn't always mean we had specified nonbinary housing options, but the coordinator would simply call nonbinary registrants to find out where they preferred to be housed. One camp I consulted with used "nonbinary, house with girls" and "nonbinary, house with boys" as an alternative to that system. There are lots of possibilities for navigating overnight accommodations, including all-gender housing, which is much simpler than most people realize.

Similarly on forms, it's important to include a nonbinary honorific if you're including Ms./Mrs./Mr. as a field. Mx. (pronounced "mix") is the most common nongendered honorific. Also, ensure that fields asking for family information use words like *parent/guardian* instead of *mother* and *father*. Lastly, for families with young transgender children, be sure to evaluate how easy it is for them to update their child's name in the church database. What about getting replacement baptismal or confirmation certificates that reflect their affirmed name? These are all access points to affirmation and inclusion.

Shifting away from the administrative side of things, let's talk about some general practices. One easy shift is to stop separating groups by boys and girls. Do you need two groups? Cool, then let's ask who likes dogs and who likes cats. Who has a birthday in the months between January and June versus July to December? Whose name starts with the letters A–M or N–Z? You get the idea. Dividing children by gender not only excludes children who identify outside of the binary and has the possibility to distresses children who are exploring their gender; it also tends to reinforce gender stereotypes and related behaviors.

This goes for adult programming too. Don't divide by male and female. If you're singing during worship, talk about higher voices or lower voices instead of men and women. In your choir, use the names of voice parts instead of gendered generalizations. This supports cisgender men and women whose voices don't fit into their assumed voice registers as well. If you're using a call-and-response liturgy, have one side of the sanctuary read one part and the other side respond. There are so many ways to divide people up that we don't need to constantly revert to gender.

Dress codes are another place we find things separated by gender. Some churches have recommended or required dress for rites like first communion and confirmation, for choir performances, or for special events. Not all clothing is appropriate for all spaces, but all clothing is appropriate for all genders. So let's make sure any dress expectations are not gendered. Here's some language: "We request participants to wear dress pants, collared shirts, skirts, or dresses for this semi-formal occasion." Be sure to include some resources in case a young person doesn't have access to clothing that makes them feel good and fit the request: "Need help deciding on or finding something to wear? Contact the youth director. They love to help!"

## FACILITIES

Facilities are usually what people think of first when it comes to inclusion but also struggle with the most because facilities can feel daunting to update without major capital improvements. While that's true, and most church buildings could benefit from major renovations to improve accessibility of all kinds, including for gender diversity, there are low-cost places to start. It is important to have an all-gender bathroom option, whether single stall or multistall. You may hear people refer to a space or bathroom as gender neutral, but all-gender is more affirming and inclusive. We don't want to neutralize anyone's gender. We want to ensure people of all genders know they are welcome. Like most gender-inclusive practices, all-gender restrooms don't just benefit gender-diverse people. They help parents with young children of a different gender who still need assistance in the bathroom. They help people of all ages who may need support or assistance in the bathroom, including older adults and people with disabilities.

If your church already has a single-use bathroom, relabel it as an all-gender bathroom. Signage matters. Opt for signs that communicate what is in the space (images of a toilet and a changing table, for instance) as opposed to signs that display figures that denote gender. Ensure your signs are clear and ADA-compliant. If your church doesn't have a single-use restroom that can be relabeled as all-gender, is there a multi-stall restroom that can be relabeled as all-gender? Some churches have taken one gendered bathroom somewhere in their building, perhaps that is less used, and designated it as all-gender. This has drawbacks depending on its placement, but it is better than nothing. It can help to have a lock on that multi-stall restroom so individuals can have more privacy if needed. Like most things, there is no singular right answer when it comes to inclusive facilities, but there are many ways to improve access and safety for people of all genders.

## YOUTH PROGRAMS

In youth programming, there are often lock-ins or retreats. It is essential that if housing is divided by gender, it is done so by gender identity. Remember, you can't know someone's gender identity unless they tell you. Parents and/or youth leaders often get caught up on body parts when the focus should be on community standards and expectations of behavior. Think about the behaviors you do and don't want and then build your community around those. No one should be seeing anyone's genitals on a youth retreat, so why don't we stop talking about them? Instead, focus on normalizing privacy for all young people and create community standards on how we behave when we're together. If you don't want youth making out with each other on retreat, then that's your standard. It has nothing to do with their respective body parts.

Safety while traveling for events or retreats is another consideration. Investigate the laws in states or countries you might visit on a trip. What is the political climate? Will your young people feel and be safe being themselves in these spaces? Families navigate this every single day. By being aware of that and proactively considering them when you make decisions, you're making it easier for that family to be a part of your program.

Sometimes ministries need to reconsider the places they've always gone if those places are no longer safe. The New Jersey Synod of the ELCA held its youth events at the same retreat center for nearly twenty years, and then that retreat center updated its contract to specify that people had to use bathrooms based on the sex they were assigned at birth. That wasn't in alignment with the New Jersey's Synod's beliefs, policies, or practices. So the Synod made the hard decision to end its relationship with that retreat center. The decision was hard in the sense that it was emotional for Synod leaders who had a longstanding relationship with the retreat center, and cutting ties is never easy. But the choice to make the decision was quite clear. The Synod's core beliefs and policies informed its actions.

Transgender and gender-expansive youth have so much to deal with today. The landscape is volatile, and they are being used as pawns in adults' political games. They need places where they can be themselves, where they can talk about what they experience, and where they can put aside the concerns of navigating the big, scary world out there. Our congregations and our youth programs can create that space for them. Let them talk about gender if they want but also let them just be kids, not always the "trans kid." The truth is transgender and gender-diverse kids are so much more than their gender identity. Get to know them, and they will make your communities and your world a brighter, more authentic place.

Think about this now before there is a child in your midst for whom you're making accommodations (although chances are there is already a child in your midst). It's unsettling to be the family that prompts the creation of policy. Do it now. Have clear gender-affirming policies rooted in your theology and approved by your leadership. Think about whether or not every person who encounters you or your church will know that transgender and nonbinary children are made in the image of God. If you're not sure, consider how you can make sure they do. From emblems of welcome like a Pride flag outside or a symbol on the door to the language you use and messages you convey, be clear about who you are so that others don't have to wonder.

## RESOURCE ORGANIZATIONS

If you as a leader or a congregation are committed to working toward the full inclusion of transgender and nonbinary people in your community, there are many resources available to you. First, if you're part of a denomination, there is likely an organization dedicated to this work. In the Lutheran church, we have ReconcilingWorks. ReconcilingWorks is an organization dedicated to the full inclusion of not just LGBTQ+ people but all people in the church and the world. In their words, "We are

Lutherans working with the recognition that racism, sexism, ageism, ableism, heterosexism, homophobia, and all the other artificial distinctions that seek to raise one group into privilege and preference over another, conspire together to diminish our world and church."[1]

ReconcilingWorks advocates for LGBTQ+ people in the church, educates around inclusion and welcome, and facilitates the Reconciling in Christ (RIC) program. In the RIC program, a church goes through a process of learning, conversation, and growth that, if all goes as planned, culminates with the adoption of a welcome statement and inclusion in the RIC directory of affirming churches. These are churches that have committed to the "welcome, inclusion, celebration and advocacy for people of all sexual orientations, gender identities and gender expressions"[2] as well as to the work of antiracism. While they may differ in structure or execution, many denominations have organizations like ReconcilingWorks. For example, Reconciling Ministries Network for the United Methodist Church and More Light Presbyterians for the Presbyterian Church (USA). Additionally, the Institute for Welcoming Resources (www.welcomingresources. org), a program of the National LGBTQ+ Task Force, provides information and tools for a more inclusive church in collaboration with partner organizations from various denominations, including those mentioned above.

Beyond possible denominational resources, consider the secular resources in your community. Find out if there are LGBTQ+ community centers nearby and if a PFLAG chapter meets in your town. These are resources that can help you in your journey and also that you can recommend to families and young people who could benefit from them. Finally, it's helpful to connect to local and state equality organizations to understand what resources they offer and how the church may be able to support their work.

It's up to you to get educated and then to educate the people in your community. Host documentary screenings or gender-expansive speakers. Provide educational material in your resource areas. Talk to your congregation about what's happening to transgender youth, why it's wrong, and what you can do to help. If this feels like it's beyond your own education, then bring in resource people. Our faith calls us to love our neighbors, and we have to learn about our neighbors to be able to do that. This will lead into the work of advocacy, but we'll get to that in a bit. Start with your own community members. Teach them and make changes together.

## THE WORK OF INCLUSION

Inclusion work needs to grow out of your theology, be articulated in your mission, and be lived out in your vision. Most importantly, this thread of celebration and inclusion needs to be sewn into the very fabric of the church. If you have a welcoming statement but don't address your facilities and your programs, you're not truly inclusive and affirming. If your forms are inclusive and the language you use in worship is intentional and affirming but you're not communicating that to the community through clear signs of welcome, the impact of your work will be limited. If your commitment toward inclusion is not integrated into every piece of your ministry from the buildings to your theology, one of two things will happen that you don't want to happen.

First and foremost, you will do harm. Transgender, nonbinary, and gender-expansive people and their families are constantly looking for clues as to whether a place is going to be safe or not. I discussed earlier in the book how parents become incredible detectives as they work to ensure their child's well-being, intentionally surrounding them with allies and advocates while hopefully protecting them from as much harm as possible. We know we can't protect them from everything, but it's our job to be diligent in the places we take our children and the people we allow into our lives. Most LGBTQ+ people navigate the world looking for signs of acceptance and inclusion, indicators of how much of ourselves we can share with any given person or place and how guarded we need to be with our hearts and our families.

So if you put out a rainbow Pride flag or publish a welcome statement, people will see these indicators of inclusion and maybe let down their guard a bit. They will breathe a sigh of relief believing that this place cares and understands enough to have inclusive practices. Then they will be crushed when their child wants to go on a youth group trip and everyone panics about sleeping arrangements or when they fill out forms for Sunday school and they're asked for their child's gender with only an option for boy or girl. They will have made themselves vulnerable, and so those things will cause more harm than if they hadn't been told that this church welcomed people of all gender identities and expressions. It's not enough to say, "We welcome all people." We need to do the work in every facet of our ministry to create spaces where all kinds of people can thrive. I'm not suggesting you can do all this work at once. It is ongoing. But we can be honest about where we're at and commit to continual learning and transformation, that same work we are called to as the body of Christ, so that our communities might better reflect the kingdom of God.

The other possible result of not doing this work in a holistic way, a way that flows from our theology and informs every single other piece of who we are as a church, is that we will give up. Inevitably on this journey toward building safer and more welcoming churches for transgender and gender-diverse young people, we will face criticism and pushback. We will hear from those who prefer "the way the church has always been" or whose political ideas are impacting their understanding of the gospel. People will threaten us with their church attendance and their stewardship dollars. They will take their toys and go home. If what you are doing isn't critical to your very identity as a person of faith or as a church, you're not going to let people and money walk away. You'll cave, or maybe you'll soften. You'll make compromises that put others in jeopardy. But if we know this work of inclusion and affirmation of transgender and gender-diverse people is directly connected to the gospel, directly connected to our mission and vision, then we have a reason to do the hard thing in front of us. We will stand firm.

## WHEN PEOPLE DISAGREE

What do we do when people disagree? Assuming our commitment to the affirmation and celebration of transgender and non-binary people is part of who we are, we know abandoning our efforts is not an option. But what is? Do we tell people to get on board or get out? Wave to them as the door shuts behind them? I don't think that's what we're called to do as a church, and thankfully, I don't think that's necessary. Instead, we get super clear about what it means to be a Christian community. We get super clear about the expectations we have for one another as siblings in Christ. These expectations are not that we all must agree, but we do need to respect each other and care for one another as God's children.

The details of what this looks like in your specific community may vary, but they can be very simple. We don't actively and intentionally harm each other. We don't call each other by names we don't consent to be called. It is not our job to judge anyone but instead our job to love one another as Christ loved us. This can be tricky territory. There are many Christians who say we are called to love and not judge while simultaneously condemning LGBTQ+ identities as sinful. It's wrapped up in the idea of "love the sinner, hate the sin." That's why your theology must unapologetically declare that transgender children are made in God's own image to be who they know themselves to be so that transgender and nonbinary people and their families understand your theological foundation. Every person in your community doesn't need to believe that, but they can't harm others in that disbelief. We don't need to be exclusive for the sake of inclusion, but we do need to set boundaries to keep those who are most vulnerable safe.

At the same time, we should consider what we mean when we say, "All are welcome." I've already explained the ways transgender and nonbinary people aren't actually welcome in many of our communities—through policy, practice, and program, through facilities and language. We've talked about ways we can become more authentically and holistically welcoming to transgender, nonbinary, and all gender-diverse people, and I also wonder if we have to decide if we truly believe all people are welcome. Are those publicly campaigning for office on platforms that dehumanize transgender and nonbinary people welcome? Are white supremacists welcome? Are people wielding weapons welcome? Are those who are spreading hateful messages on social media about vulnerable children of God welcome? I've suggested we manage our differences through clear expectations in community. *You can't say those things here. You can't bring your weapons here. You can't treat people badly here.* But is it okay if the local politician publicly spreads horrible lies about transgender people every other day of the week but behaves politely on Sunday? Is it okay for members to be active in hate groups if they don't say anything about it on Sunday mornings? The presence of some people, regardless of how they abide by our boundaries and expectations, makes vulnerable communities unsafe. What do we do then? Are all welcome?

I don't have answers for you. I mean, I have my answer, but you have to figure out what the answer is for you and for your community. For me, if your presence harms another member of the community, then maybe you aren't welcome in this particular expression of the church. Are you loved by God? Absolutely. Are you a part of the body of Christ? Yes. Is there limitless love and grace available to you? You betcha. But that doesn't mean you get to be a part of this community. Is that being exclusive for the sake of inclusion? Maybe. I don't know. But I will always err on the side of protecting the most vulnerable in our midst.

As a community, you need to figure out what this means for you. What are your boundaries? How will you make decisions about who is included when you say, "All are welcome," and how will you hold yourselves accountable to making sure that what you say is true? May these conversations be guided by the Holy Spirit and filled with generative conflict that helps us get clearer about who we are as children of God and what that means for how we're called to show up in the world.

## FINAL THOUGHTS

Pastor, faith leader, or youth director,

Please know that if someone handed you this book or this chapter, it's because they believe in you. They have put their hope in you, and that hope is for a church that will love a lot louder, that will unequivocally celebrate and care for the transgender and gender-diverse children in their midst. They are hoping you'll be a part of making that happen.

I want families to know they don't have to choose between their child and their faith, but they absolutely may have to choose between their child and their church. If you're not willing to show up and do the work, if you can't keep this child in your midst reasonably safe, then please be honest. Point them in the direction of someone who can and send them on their way. Then get back to work in your community so you'll be ready for the next family. These children and their well-being and their lives matter far more than your attendance numbers. It's not about you. It's a God thing, and sometimes the best thing we can do is get out of the way.

If someone trusts you with their story, hold it carefully. Remember, when someone comes out to you, they come out to only you. That information is precious and only to be shared with their explicit permission. Thank them and ask them how you can best help.

They may not have the answers, but I trust that together with the Holy Spirit moving among you, you will create spaces where more people can show up in the fullness of who God created them to be, and when they do, beautiful and holy things happen.

Until then, thank you from this mama of a transgender kiddo turned teenager who dreams of a church where she doesn't have to teach people why her identity is not a mistake but a beautiful gift from the God who knows and loves her.

# 11 | COLLECTIVE LIBERATION

This chapter is something I knew needed to be written and the thing I felt the least qualified to write. As someone who is constantly learning from and listening to people who know more about this than I do—primarily BIPOC advocates, educators, and thought leaders—and as someone who has done enough work to know I'll never have done enough work, writing this was intimidating. (BIPOC stands for Black, Indigenous, and people of color.) I don't say this to elicit sympathy, absolutely not. I share it because it's true. Being raised in a society built on white supremacy has taught me that I should be able to know and understand all things, that I should belong everywhere, and that all things belong to me. I don't rationally believe these things, but it's embedded in white American colonizing culture. When talking about antiracism and the experiences of Black and brown people in this country, I have to get real about the fact that I won't ever know and understand all the things. I don't get to be an expert, and this conversation doesn't belong to me. And yet, also, I have a deep responsibility to use my voice and privilege as a white person to actively dismantle the white supremacist systems of oppression and power.

Knowing I wouldn't get this right on the first try, I asked my friend Maya May, a Black mother to a transgender child, to read it. And y'all, I got it wrong. In staying with the structure of the rest of the book, I started with a story from my own experiences. Doing so unintentionally centered my family. This chapter is different from the rest of the book, and that didn't belong there. I trust Maya to call me on what I refer to as my "white lady nonsense." (I admittedly use a more colorful word than *nonsense*.) To be clear, it's my responsibility to do my own work; it can't be on Maya. But Maya also knows I'm doing that work, and so when she has the bandwidth, she trusts me to receive her feedback and do something generative with it. I also have white accountability partners with whom I can work through things so that I don't unnecessarily ask for the labor of a person of color.

The truth is I am having these conversations in every area of my life right now. These conversations are happening in the church, in LGBTQ+ advocacy organizations, and they are most certainly happening in my personal circles. As with everything we've covered in this book so far, we don't have to have all the answers, but we need to learn and do the work. Most importantly, we need to normalize taking in new information and allowing ourselves and our actions to be transformed.

## CONNECTIONS

The work we do in advocacy, the work we do in creating gender-inclusive spaces, isn't just about transgender and nonbinary youth. There are expanding circles of impact. When we fight for and work to build a world that is safe for transgender and nonbinary youth, we must also fight for all LGBTQ+ youth. And when we fight for LGBTQ+ youth, we must fight for youth who have been historically excluded and intentionally marginalized in a multitude of ways. I'm going to rely heavily on the wisdom of Black feminists and transgender people of color in this chapter because they have been doing this work before I even knew this work existed. While it is my responsibility to use my voice and privilege in our work toward education and justice, it is not my place to suggest I am an expert or that I have any of this figured out. I'm forever a student, learning from and being transformed by these leaders, and I humbly put my energy and efforts into the movement created by them and their ancestors.

I've already said the work of gender inclusion benefits all people in breaking down barriers and limitations rooted in gender norms, but we must go a bit further. In the end, this work we're doing is about disrupting hundreds of years of systems of power and oppression—racism and white supremacy, sexism and patriarchy, colonialism, ableism, and more. If that's not what we're doing, then we're failing our kids. It's all connected.

It's all connected because we're all connected. We are parts of the body of Christ, unique in experiences, gifts, and struggles but still united in one body: "If one member suffers, all suffer together with it; if one member is honored, all rejoice together with it" (1 Cor. 12:26). We cannot seek justice for just one part of the body to stop our collective suffering. We are interdependent on one another, and our collective liberation depends on the liberation of those who are most oppressed, most marginalized.

Of course, the body of Christ metaphor is not as simple as it may appear. Our natural tendency to sort and categorize things based on their commonalities gets in the way when we're talking about human beings in all their complexity. We think we can assign parts to types of people. Transgender people are this part; cisgender people are that part. Men are this part; women are that part. White people are one part; Black people are another. But there are white transgender men and Black transgender women. These identities can't be separated out and compartmentalized.

Each of us contains a multitude of identities and layers that make up who we are and impact how we experience the world. Furthermore, if we exclude transgender people, for example, we're not just missing a piece of a hand or a foot. Our friends in the disability community remind us that you can be a whole person without a foot or an arm. Instead, we're missing indefinable yet integral pieces of *every* part of the body. This means when we exclude or marginalize people and communities based on gender identity, race, ability, or anything else, we don't just lose a part of the body; we lose something greater. We're all needed to make up the body of Christ, not just in our parts but in our wholeness. We can't work toward the liberation of one piece of a human being and expect them to be free. We have to strive for holistic liberation.

## PIECES OF IDENTITY

I'm a white woman of European descent. I am a citizen of the country where I live, and my parents and grandparents were raised here. I am a cisgender queer person who often feels constrained by the binary. I'm married to a man, so people perceive me as straight. I don't have a visible disability, and I live with anxiety and depression. I was baptized Lutheran as a baby and have always been part of the Lutheran Church. I'm a child of divorced parents, neither of whom graduated from college but were always employed. I've experienced food and housing insecurity, but my basic needs were always somehow met. I co-parent my three children with my spouse. As I write this, I am sitting on land that is part of the traditional territory of the Lenni-Lenape people, called Lenapehoking.[1] There is more to who I am, but these are some pieces of my identity that impact the way I experience the world.

In the same way, transgender and nonbinary people have more than one piece of their identity. In their own words, here is what a few transgender people have to say about their identities:

"I am Black, and I am trans, and I am masculine all at the same time. When I walk into a room, I bring all of those things with me. There's not one thing that is more important than the other, and I can't just shed one of those things."—Tiq Milan[2]

"What people highlight about your identity shifts depending on the environment you're in. That's true with anyone. I'm definitely all of the above [trans, deaf, and Chinese], but I'm also creative, passionate, empathetic, goofy, tired, sometimes hungry. I'm a lot of different things, but one of those won't ever rise above. I just am all those things."
—Chella Man[3]

"Today I stand here as a queer Black transgender woman from Augusta, [Georgia]. But I am more [than] these labels. I am also a daughter, a sister, an auntie, a friend, a lover, a human, a feminist."—Raquel Willis[4]

"I am a trans woman of color, and that identity has enabled me to be true to myself, offering an anchor from which I can uplift my visible blackness, my often-invisible trans womanhood, my little-talked-about native Hawaiian heritage, and the many iterations of womanhood they combine. When I think of identity, I think of our bodies and souls and the influences of family, culture, and community—the ingredients that make us."—Janet Mock[5]

Yes, they are transgender, and they are so many other things. No one's identity can or should be reduced to a single part of them. Because there are Black transgender youth, disabled transgender youth, transgender youth who are refugees or who are experiencing food and housing insecurity, when we fight for transgender justice, we must also be fighting for racial justice, disability justice, gender justice, economic justice, and so much more. We must work toward justice for all people.

## INTERSECTIONALITY AND PRIVILEGE

Still, we need to go even deeper. In 1989, legal scholar Kimberlé Crenshaw introduced the term *intersectionality* in her essay "Demarginalizing the Intersection of Race and Sex."[6] She explained the limits of antidiscrimination laws to address the lived realities of Black women because "the intersectional experience is greater than the sum of racism and sexism." The oppression of Black women couldn't be fully addressed without considering the intersections of their identities. It's not as simple as one plus one equals two; instead, the layers of our identities impact our experience in the world, exponentially increasing our oppression or our privilege. Many of us hold some privileged identities and some oppressed identities. For example, my daughter Rebekah benefits from white privilege but is marginalized as a transgender person. Both of these are valid; they don't negate each other.

And her experience of oppression as a transgender person is very different from that of a Black or brown transgender person. Her relative experience of privilege and oppression doesn't make her better or worse than anyone else, more or less valuable, but it does impact the way she navigates the world. When we recognize our relative privilege in any area, we can use it to work toward justice.

I think people struggle with the concept of privilege because they hear the world telling them they have privilege in a certain area and think it means the world thinks they "have it easy." That's not how it works. As a white person, you may experience oppression and deep struggle related to your socioeconomic status, being disabled, or a variety of other things. You still have white privilege because you don't experience systematic oppression related to your race. Similarly, a person of color can have a variety of other points of privilege—economic, ability, citizenship, and more. They also experience oppression because they are a person of color. Like most things in this book, it's far more complicated and nuanced than many see at first glance.

In 1977, a decade before Kimberlé Crenshaw introduced the term *intersectionality*, a group of Black feminists known as the Combahee River Collective introduced the idea of identity politics. They described identity politics as not a tool of separation but one of empowered action rooted in their own unique experiences and their desire for liberation; it's a far cry from the way the term is understood today. Alicia Garza, cofounder of the international Black Lives Matter movement, writes, "For the Combahee River Collective, their life experiences were shaped by what they called 'interlocking oppressions'—racism, sexism, capitalism, heterosexism, and the like. They committed themselves to being anti-racist, unlike their white counterparts, and anti-sexist, unlike their white and Black male counterparts. . . . They sought political spaces that would allow for the complexity of their experiences as Black, as Black women, as Black women who were lesbians."[7] Interlocking oppression, the unique overlap of their identities and their subordination, again helps us understand both how each of us is more than the sum of our parts and how that impacts the lives we lead and the discrimination we may or may not face.

## WHITE SUPREMACY

Let's take a moment to acknowledge the way Black feminists have led and continue to lead the way in the fight for justice and a holistic understanding of equity despite being pushed to the margins again and again. Like many white people, I had no idea how much I didn't know, and despite everything I've learned over the better part of the last decade, I still know I have so much to learn. Garza writes, "In the United States, white people, white culture, and white experiences are the control against everything else is compared."[8] Remember how the continuum for gender identity, gender expression, and sexual orientation was problematic because it limited us to defining ourselves in relation to the norm found in the binary boxes of male and female, man and woman? Well, whiteness functions in the same way, except it is arguably more toxic because instead of a continuum or even a binary, it's the singular standard by which things are judged, unconsciously or consciously.

Even as we've talked throughout this book about societal expectations of gender in the United States, we must recognize that our society is rooted in white culture. I actually caught myself using *societal* and *cultural* interchangeably because for me, as a white Christian person in this country, they are largely the same. In the same way, I, as a cisgender person, never had to reflect on my gender identity because it aligned with what society told me. That's what we mean when we talk about dominant identities and the privilege they provide. I've tried to be clear that the experiences of families and young people who transition will vary based on the familial context, cultural background, and the way each of them experiences the world.

That includes race. It also includes ability, neurotypicality, citizenship, primary language, and more. It certainly includes religious background. This book is definitively written from a Christian faith perspective; specifically my perspective is that of progressive or mainline Protestant Christianity. If you are coming from a nondenominational, Catholic, Baptist, or other faith background, that will impact your experience of gender and sexuality in comparison to mine. Again, it's all connected. Our identities and experiences are far more complex than the neat little boxes in which we're consciously or unconsciously trying to fit. The gender binary is harmful and limiting, yes, and so is white supremacy. We have to disrupt both.

## HISTORY OF THE LGBTQ+ MOVEMENT

The LGBTQ+ movement has struggled to do both of those things for a long time. The movement has silenced and, until recently, refused to acknowledge the transgender women of color crucial to its inception. Marsha P. Johnson was a Black gay liberation activist and self-identified drag queen. (The term *transgender* wasn't popularized until after her death; Johnson did use the word *transvestite* to describe herself. Historians and Johnson's former friends often refer to her as transgender.) Sylvia Rivera was a Latina transgender woman. Both were on the front lines of the Stonewall Uprising in 1969, when police raided the Stonewall Inn, a gay bar in Greenwich Village.

In the days and years that followed, Johnson and Rivera organized the growing gay rights movement. Meanwhile, gay rights leaders were resistant to including transgender people in their advocacy. Inspired by their own experiences of violence and discrimination, Johnson and Rivera focused on organizing for the most vulnerable, founding Street Transvestite Action Revolutionaries (STAR) in 1970. STAR worked to protect and support those the larger gay rights movement were ignoring, especially young people who were transgender, LGBTQ+, and/or living on the street. Fifty years after Stonewall, Rivera and Johnson have just begun to be recognized by the wider movement, and transgender women of color continue to fight for their voices to be heard while they continue to experience the highest rates of violence.[9] Even in the telling of Rivera and Johnson's stories, Black transgender voices continue to be erased. Netflix's 2017 documentary *The Death and Life of Marsha P. Johnson* faced criticism when it was released, as director David France failed to credit the extensive work of Black transgender filmmaker and activist Tourmaline, who had been researching and archiving the lives of Johnson and Rivera for years.[10] So much of what those early revolutionaries faced continues to be reality for transgender women of color today.

Raquel Willis, a writer, editor, and activist, speaks honestly about her experience as a Black transgender woman in the fight for gender equality. In her remarks at the January 2017 Women's March, she said, "Although I'm glad to be here now, it's disheartening that women like me were an afterthought in the initial planning of this march. Many of us had to stand a little taller to be heard, and that exclusion is nothing new. . . . As we commit to each other to build this movement of resistance and liberation, *no one* can be an afterthought. We have a chance to be stronger and better than we ever have before—and that starts with having hard conversations and being held accountable."[11]

Janet Mock reflected on beginning to speak out about the inequity and injustice she saw in the movement: "My awakening pushed me to be more vocal about these issues, prompting uncomfortable but necessary conversations about the movement privileging middle- and upper-class cis, gay, and lesbian rights over the daily access issues plaguing low-income queer and trans youth and LGBT people of color, communities that carry interlocking identities that are not mutually exclusive, that make them all the more vulnerable to poverty, homelessness, unemployment, HIV/AIDS, hyper-criminalization, violence, and so much more."[12]

The themes are obvious. The movement must stop centering those most privileged and instead focus on those most marginalized. Crenshaw suggested in her 1989 essay that if we focus on "addressing the needs and problems of those who are most disadvantaged . . . restructuring and remaking the world where necessary, then others who are singularly disadvantaged would also benefit."[13] Biblically, we can get behind this. Our faith calls us to do the same. Matthew 25:40 reminds us, "Truly I tell you, just as you did it to one of the least of these [siblings] of mine, you did it to me."

Of course, as Mock and Willis both note, we must be willing to have hard or uncomfortable conversations and be held accountable. Our impact matters, regardless of our intent. While we may not have been raised to know the work that needs to be done, people have been trying to tell us for decades. Just as we can commit to learning and doing the work around celebrating the transgender and gender-diverse children in our lives, we can commit to learning and doing the work around other identities. And just like when it comes to gender, we're going to make mistakes along the way.

## TETHERING OUR ROWBOATS

As a white woman in this space, I *definitely* don't always get this right. I never will. But I keep trying. In the same way that we cannot say "not all Christians" to excuse ourselves from the harm done by people who share this identity with us, we cannot say "not all white people" and excuse ourselves from the harm of racism or any other ism. Much like the assumptions and beliefs we have around gender are so ingrained in who we are and how we've been raised that it takes ongoing intentional work to shift them, racism is part of how we view the world. It's in our institutions, our media, and our standards of beauty. It's everywhere. I feel like I eat, sleep, and breathe work around gender inclusion, and sometimes I'm still surprised by a thought or something that comes out of my mouth that goes against everything I believe and work for. That's because those old beliefs are deeply embedded into my brain. It's been in the air I've breathed since I was born. I can't escape that; I simply have to keep working to identify it and remove it. The same is true for racism and white supremacy.

As I work with LGBTQ+ advocates and organizations across the country in the fight for equity and justice, I am grateful for another friend who reminds me of the bigger picture. Lizette Trujillo is a Chicanx parent of a transgender son. She consistently calls me into hard conversations and holds me accountable and capable. She regularly reminds me and other advocates in this space that we have to tether our rowboats together.

She wrote, "Every mechanism of systemic racism that was created to keep Black, indigenous, and people of color oppressed are the same mechanisms used to harm LGBTQIA people regardless of their race. Throughout history, we have seen each marginalized group move and push towards justice, each movement a rowboat trying to break past that wave of bias and discrimination. But what we must do is tether our boats together to ensure we achieve true progress and equality. Your fight is my fight, and together we can create change and progress in a way that uplifts us all."[14]

Lizette has taught me that if each of us working toward justice of some kind is in our own small but sturdy rowboat, it's us against the storm. It's our tiny rowboat against the huge waves of oppression, of systems of power, of discrimination. But we don't have to go it alone. We're sailing through the same storm; we're all fighting for liberation. If we can tether our rowboats together, building coalitions in our work and shifting our focus to our collective liberation, we are safer and more powerful. Put simply, liberation isn't possible unless it's collective.

It's probably time I remind you: breathe deep, make space, take a step. We're not going to figure this all out right now. We're learning together. We're heading in the same direction. We are not called to be perfect. We're called to love, grace, and the work of justice. There's some reading recommendations in the back of the book if you want to learn more. I'll say the same thing Lizette did. Your fight is my fight. Together, we can create change. And, I'll add, we can care for one another in the process.

# 12 | THE SCARY TRANSGENDER PERSON

Rebekah was ten years old the first time she carried a protest sign; it said, "I'm the Scary Transgender Person the Media Warned You About." She was only ten years old the first time she spoke to a crowd gathered in the streets to defend her rights to access a safe and supportive educational environment. She stood there in her pink puffy coat with her pink hair braided into pigtails asking a crowd of two hundred people to come together and fight for equality. It was 2017, and the federal administration had just rescinded the guidance for transgender students in schools. Rebekah didn't necessarily understand everything that meant, but she understood that it made kids like her less safe.

Since then, things have gotten worse: the year 2022 was the worst legislative year on record for the LGBTQ+ community, and transgender children were the most common target. At the start of 2023, at least eight states had already prefiled anti-trans bills ahead of their upcoming state legislative sessions.[1] Each year, on November 20, we observe Transgender Day of Remembrance, honoring those lives lost in the preceding year. Each year, we say the names of dozens of people who were killed because they were transgender. The year 2021 was the deadliest year on record for transgender people, with more than forty-six individuals being murdered in acts of anti-trans violence. When I mentioned before that transgender people don't struggle because of who they are but because of what they face in society, this is what I mean.

We're living in a time when we must hold greater awareness and visibility than ever before in tension with increasingly aggressive legislative attacks, ongoing violence, and a cultural war centered on transgender people and their bodies. *Time* magazine coined the phrase *the transgender tipping* point in a May 2014 issue featuring Laverne Cox on the cover. The idea was that we had reached a critical mass of representation and visibility of transgender people in the media and the world. Transgender people had stepped into popular culture in a way we'd never before seen. The backlash was fierce. With the Obama administration in the White House, we saw the highest places in the US government include and celebrate transgender people for the first time. The growing awareness of transgender people made them a topic of debate everywhere from family dinner tables to state legislatures as bathroom bills (bills that would police or prohibit transgender people from using the bathroom that aligns with their gender identity) were introduced. Caitlyn Jenner came out in April 2015, further intensifying the national conversation around transgender people, with most folks unable to separate their feelings about Caitlyn Jenner as a person from their feelings about the community as a whole.

Gavin Grimm, a transgender high school student from Virginia, sued his school with the support of the ACLU[2] to gain access to the boys' bathrooms. When Gavin initially transitioned, he was permitted to the use the boys' bathrooms and did so for seven weeks without incident until local parents and community members mobilized in outrage, leading the school board to adopt a policy that required students to use facilities that aligned with their sex assigned at birth. In May 2016, I wept when the Departments of Justice and Education released guidance for transgender students in schools clarifying that Title IX, a federal law protecting students from discrimination on the basis of sex, protects transgender students. This wasn't a change in law but a powerful explanation of the law that already existed. Two months later, Sarah McBride spoke at the 2016 Democratic National Convention, becoming the first openly transgender person to speak at a national party convention, and I watched as my daughter saw herself represented on that stage. She may not have known exactly what it meant, but she knew it was a big deal.

## PLATFORM AND PRIVILEGE

We celebrated huge leaps in visibility and acceptance, while simultaneously transgender rights were becoming a major political sticking point in the battles between Republicans and Democrats leading up to the 2016 election. As it was for many, November 8, 2016, was a night I'll never forget. A sign of my own privilege, I had never before been afraid for my family's safety as the result of an election. We lived in an overwhelmingly conservative area, and the messaging around the election had been hard. I shook with fear and anger reading parents in local Facebook groups debate transgender students' right to access bathrooms, not knowing that my daughter used the bathroom with their children every day. The things they said were dehumanizing and violent; it was terrifying.

In the months leading up to the election, we became even more acutely aware of the people around us, what they believed, and what that meant for our family's safety. I put Rebekah to sleep on November 8, our future uncertain, and she begged to not have to leave the house ever again if Trump won. I hugged her and told her everything would be okay, even though I wasn't sure. Then after I quietly closed her door behind me, the tears came. For hours, I cried and watched ongoing election results alone in my room. A friend came over to watch with us, but I couldn't bring myself to go downstairs. My stomach hurt as I sobbed, trying to figure out how to tell my little girl that the country she lived in had voted for a person who didn't believe that she should be protected or supported in being herself in the world.

We all know how that election ended, and the years that followed would prove our fears warranted in so many ways. In February 2017, the Trump administration rescinded the guidance for transgender students in schools. While New Jersey had an antidiscrimination law that protected people on the basis of gender identity, the confusion that ensued from the media and the headlines deeply impacted students everywhere. The message was clear: the White House did not support transgender students. I reached out to Garden State Equality, an organization I had begun working with, and offered to speak at a rally they were organizing. They called me back and said, "Yeah, you and your daughter can speak." She was just ten years old. I almost said no, but then I realized I needed to give her the choice. It was her identity, after all. She said yes. Her school experience had been really positive, and she believed all students deserved that. She spoke, standing next to me, in the streets of Jersey City in front of two hundred people and told her story. I posted a picture of her with her sign, the sign she'd stayed up late the night before to make that said, "I'm the Scary Transgender Person the Media Warned You About," on social media. It went viral.

Interview requests suddenly flooded my inbox—*Teen Vogue*, Yahoo News, *Huffington Post*. She was still just ten years old, but something powerful happened at that rally. More powerful than her speaking out for the first time was her hearing the stories of other transgender people, young and not so young. These stories weren't as positive as hers. They hadn't had the privilege of being put in the protective bubble that we had somehow managed. They had struggled at home, at school, and into adulthood. This was the first time she realized that not all transgender people are surrounded by love and support, that they experience alarming rates of discrimination, rejection, harassment, and abuse. So when the media started calling, she said yes. Suddenly, we had a platform, and she was ready to use it.

No child should have to defend their right to exist, but all too often, transgender and gender-expansive kids must do just that. They are forced to advocate for themselves at home, in school, and at church. They have been turned into political footballs used to rally voters around fear. Families with transgender children are harassed and reported for child abuse. When Rebekah was eleven years old, we had our first visit from Child Protective Services. We tried to explain that people had reported us for supporting our transgender child, but the staff just didn't understand. They said, "Why would someone make a false report saying you're forcing your child to be a girl?" I think most good people would wonder the same thing. Unfortunately, the tactic is used to silence families like ours who speak out and advocate for all transgender kids. I'll talk more about this later in this chapter.

Gavin Grimm's case went through a series of decisions and appeals all the way up to the Supreme Court, only to be sent back down to the lower court when the Trump administration's Department of Education withdrew its support from the case. Eventually, sometime after Gavin was no longer a high school student, he would win his case, and the Supreme Court would refuse to hear the appeal, ending the case for good. But the court battles for transgender and LGBTQ+ rights continue. The rollercoaster of progress and backlash continues.

## VISIBILITY AND VULNERABILITY

Visibility is a powerful but dangerous thing. In the past few years, Pride, an event that started with a riot against police violence in 1969 at the Stonewall Inn in New York City, has gone corporate. June is filled with what the community has named *rainbow capitalism*, companies cashing in on their supposed acceptance and inclusion by selling rainbow products and plastering their names all over Pride parades and events. Meanwhile, many of those same companies continue to support elected officials who are doing egregious harm to the LGBTQ+ community.

In 2022, representation in media was at an all-time high. We are finally seeing films and television series that include positive and realistic portrayals of transgender people played by transgender people. We still have a long way to go, but we're moving away from exclusively showing transgender people with tropes and trauma. Books telling the stories of transgender and gender-diverse people are slowly making their way into schools and libraries across the country. Of course, that comes with its own backlash. Calls to boycott media companies and efforts to ban books are raging, with Florida's "Don't Say Gay" bill, passed and signed into law in 2021, being one of the most prominent examples. In reality, "Don't Say Gay" is one piece of a much bigger plan.

The current attacks on transgender young people are coordinated. If you were to look at the anti-trans bills introduced across the country, you might be surprised to find that many of them read the same, practically word for word. These bills are based off model legislation supplied by national groups like American Legislative Exchange Council (ALEC) and Alliance Defending Freedom (ADF), and the efforts to get these bills passed are supported by these same groups and others like the Heritage Foundation and the Family Research Council.[3] These organizations are deeply connected to and funded by the religious right. Previously relying largely on religious arguments, they are shifting their focus to isolating transgender people from the larger progressive community with the goal of dividing coalitions, including feminists and LGBTQ+ people. Divide and conquer. Stop diversity and equity efforts to stay in power. That's the goal, and they've discovered transgender youth are the vulnerable link to help them do it. Meanwhile, most people still say they don't know a transgender person, so they have no personal experience to counteract the politically driven misinformation they're hearing.[4]

Politicians need to convince people to care about things in order to get them to vote. Fear is the most powerful tool to do that. So they incite fear about transgender and gender-diverse people, suggesting they are threats to our children, our families, and our society. They are doing so relentlessly and effectively. In 2022, we saw states attempt to ban transgender children from K–12 athletics, with eighteen states enacting laws banning these athletes. A number of states also attempted to ban transgender health care for minors, with four states signing restrictions on affirming health care into law. Plus, there are ongoing efforts to criminalize parents who support their children and to destabilize families.

These efforts are nothing short of attempts to eradicate transgender people from society. If they cannot use the bathroom safely, if they cannot access the health care that allows them to survive and even thrive, if they cannot be full participants in schools and communities, if their families are torn apart and their access to necessary resources are denied, trans people will not be able to continue to exist. Some will try to be people they aren't. Some will be unable to go on living. And still others will remove themselves from community and culture as much as possible to protect themselves.

## BECAUSE OF OUR FAITH

The only thing stable in the political and cultural landscape around transgender and nonbinary people is instability. I don't know where we'll be as of the publication of this book. And I don't know where we'll be three years after that. What I do know is that this uncertainty around transgender rights and acceptance is certain to continue. Advocates are fighting relentlessly in the courts, and community organizers and educators are working to implement policy and practices that support transgender people in all areas of life. Chase Strangio, deputy director for Transgender Justice with the ACLU's LGBT and HIV Project, says that our liberation will not be found in the court system. He says it's necessary damage control, but there is no point where these fights end.[5] Our liberation must come from community, from radical organizing and mutual aid, from radical acceptance, inclusion, and celebration of transgender people in a way that subverts society's systems of power and oppression, destroys the restrictions of the gender binary, and, in my humble opinion, looks more like the kingdom of God than anything we've seen before.

What does this all mean? First and foremost, pastors and lay leaders need to know that people of faith do the most egregious harm to transgender and nonbinary people, personally and politically. And it is people of faith who are most essential to stopping that harm and repairing the damage. It's not enough to create safe spaces in our homes and churches because transgender and nonbinary kids live out in the world. Transgender and nonbinary people and their families need to hear faith communities boldly, loudly, and joyfully proclaim that transgender and nonbinary people are holy. This needs to be clearly and consistently communicated through every part of your work.

We must speak out, not in spite of our faith but because of it. In response to God's love, our faith calls us to lift each other up and work to stop suffering. We can do that directly in our communities, but the work doesn't stop there. God calls us out into the world to dismantle unjust systems of power and protect the most vulnerable. That call includes fighting for dignity, equity, and justice for all transgender and nonbinary young people. The Bible and the Christian faith are being used as the foundation on which to ban and marginalize these young people. If that doesn't align with our faith, and I would certainly argue that it doesn't, we have to speak out about what our faith says or be complicit in the harm being done. We are complicit if we do not speak as loudly and urgently in support of transgender and nonbinary young people as others are speaking against them. This isn't about saying, "Well, not all Christians . . . ," to defend ourselves. It's about changing the dominant narrative around Christianity and transgender people. It's about disrupting the power and control those Christians have over our faith and our country.

Data has shown over the years that Christians who support protections for LGBTQ+ people outnumber those who don't,[6] but you'd never know it when you listen to the national conversation. Just like Tor's experience in their congregation growing up, most people assume the worst when it comes to Christians and the LGBTQ+ community. The loudest voices craft the narrative. As a result, young people like Tor and their families believe they must choose either their faith and their identity or their faith and their child. It's not true, and people of faith are the only ones who can set the record straight. It's time to show up.

## WHAT DOES THIS MEAN FOR FAMILIES?

Our family has been very public with our advocacy. After Rebekah transitioned, our circles of advocacy and education just got wider and wider. After Rebekah went viral, things moved quickly, and we did our best to make the decisions that felt right for Rebekah and our family at the time. The learning curve was steep. Looking back, there are things we might not have done or things we might have done differently, but we felt compelled to act.

Rebekah is protected by layers of privilege. She has two loving and educated parents who support her. She is white and generally gender conforming. Although she advocates that we get rid of the boxes that we force boys and girls into, she generally fits into the box society has for girls her age. She goes through her daily life without people necessarily perceiving her as transgender. Plus, we live in New Jersey, a state with nondiscrimination laws and policies. All these things make our family statistically less at risk when we step into the public eye than other families. That's why we chose to do it.

That doesn't mean there aren't risks and challenges. There are many. Some we're aware of now, and some we may find out many years down the road. The most significant thing we've risked is Rebekah's privacy. She's publicly known by her real name and her image and likeness all over the internet, and as we've all heard before, the internet is forever. We can't take that back. Rebekah can never be stealth; she can never just live as the girl she knows herself to be without people being able to find out she's transgender. When we made the decision to share her story with the world, we vaguely understood this risk, but we felt it was a risk worth taking to hopefully build a world where Rebekah wouldn't ever want or need to hide her identity.

After the past five years of extremely public advocacy, I can say we're pretty far from building that world. We're not stopping anytime soon, but there will be risk for a long time to come. I do not necessarily regret our choice, but I know there is potential for Rebekah to regret our choice, that the decision she made when she was ten, twelve, or even fifteen may not be the decision she will wish she had made when she is twenty-five. I can't do anything about that, but I can caution you.

I have listened and learned from enough transgender adults who deeply believe in protecting transgender youth's privacy, especially their real name, so that their futures aren't determined by their present to urge you to do whatever you can to protect your child's privacy. Deeply consider where you use their real name. Proceed with caution with every advocacy opportunity. Don't overshare. Don't divulge the intimate details of your child's experience in an effort to change the world. There are too many people who want to exploit our children's trauma for entertainment, for something sometimes called *trauma porn*. That doesn't serve your child, first and foremost, but it also doesn't serve the greater work toward liberation. When we only learn about people from their trauma, we don't see them as human beings who, like us, deserve equity and justice. Instead, we feel sorry for them. Pity is a far cry from the solidarity that comes with shared humanity.

Guard your child's birth name with everything you have. Do not share it. Seal the name-change orders. Even if you think that it's everywhere because you used it for so long, immediately stop using it and sharing it. Go back through your social media platforms and remove it. Protect whatever privacy and dignity you can offer them moving forward. If you choose to speak publicly, if you choose to testify at legislative hearings, learn about what is part of the public record. Use pseudonyms or fake addresses. Google yourself and see what you can find and then do what you can to get any personally identifying information removed. If your child wants to speak publicly, consider the impact to their mental and emotional well-being. Consider their safety.

So many families come up to me at events because they have seen how we have been public, and they ask for help to do the same. They honestly and ardently want to work toward our children's collective liberation, and for that I am deeply grateful. But I need you to know you don't have to be on the news, on social media, or on television to do that. There is so much work to be done in our homes, our communities, our schools, and our faith spaces. And beyond that, the single most powerful act of advocacy families can engage in is loving, supporting, and protecting the child in front of you at all costs. By raising young people who are loved, supported, and empowered, we are changing the world. We will watch them change the world.

All that being true, public advocacy has been an enormous gift to our family. It's hard and scary, but we have connected with community that helps us keep going. Rebekah has discovered the power of her voice and confidence in her story. And we've been able to see glimpses of the unimaginable impact we've had on other young people. No matter how you choose to approach your advocacy, if we focus on community, empowerment, and impact as we raise these children, the world will be forever changed by our families.

## CHILD PROTECTIVE SERVICES

One of the things we were told to do when Rebekah transitioned involved a safe folder. I briefly mentioned it earlier. A safe folder is a collection of documents attesting to your child's gender nonconformity, expression of themselves, their well-being, and your competent parenting along the way. This collection of documents is intended for use if or when questions of abuse arise related to your parenting. The intention of these documents is to prove that you are a good parent, that supporting and affirming your child is an example of that good parenting, and that you are in no way forcing your children to identify apart from the sex they were assigned at birth.

Various mentors in the parenting communities along with our therapist encouraged us to start a safe folder. We heard stories of families who had their children taken away by Child Protective Services after being reported by family members or neighbors. We heard stories of parents who lost their children to a nonaffirming parent in custody court battles. Every story was terrifying and heart wrenching, yes, and we honestly thought it was unlikely to ever impact us. We live in New Jersey, a state with affirming and protective policies, and we predominantly received support from our friends and family around Rebekah's transition. Nevertheless, I put together a few basic documents—a letter from her therapist, her legal name-change documentation, and a few of her report cards that indicated a thriving child—and then I promptly forgot about it. I forgot about it for years, until the day workers from New Jersey's Division of Child Protection and Permanency (DCPP) showed up at our door.

I wasn't home. I was attending a performance of *Beauty and the Beast*, the musical Rebekah was performing in with the local community theater company. She was a singing fork and a villager; she even had a tiny solo. Someone who had likely never met us reported us, anonymously and from a blocked phone number, for forcing our son to be a girl. They used her birth name. They said she was seven years old when she was actually ten, and they said we were forcing her to take hormones (something she wouldn't take for years to come as medically appropriate) to "make her into a girl."

My husband explained to them that our daughter was transgender and her name had been legally changed to Rebekah. The two men were confused. They said, "Well, then, why would someone call this in?" My husband patiently explained our public advocacy and the backlash we'd received. The two men were still confused. They said, "Okay, but still why would someone call making this accusation?" My husband, still patiently, bless his heart, further explained that, at best, these people believe children cannot be transgender, and so it could only be a result of abuse. They said, "Oh. So they're just ignorant." Yeah, something like that. But there is nothing small or minor about their ignorance. This is a tactic being used by the far right to silence those of us speaking out for transgender rights.

DCPP came on a Saturday and said they'd be in touch on Monday. I spent the next forty-eight hours struggling to breathe, cleaning every surface, preparing for someone to enter my home and assess my parenting, and scrambling for every document I knew we had that could prove my child was in good health, was well cared for, and was, in fact, transgender, all while trying to maintain a sense of normalcy and calm for our family.

When I explained to my children that someone would be coming to the house to look around and ask us questions, I saw the look of terror on my transgender child's face. Before I even said the words, she knew someone had reported us. No matter how much I tried to tell her everything was okay, I still found myself holding her while she cried, deeply worried the state would take her away from us because of who she is and our support for her.

When they asked for releases to speak to my child's doctors and find out details about her care in order to "ensure she was receiving the appropriate medical care," I wondered how the state thought it knew more about care for transgender children than the Gender Clinic at Children's Hospital of Philadelphia, a hospital ranked fourth in the nation for best children's hospitals.[7] When they asked my kid if she was really a girl, I'm not sure they realized the depth of pain that caused a child who has fought to articulate and be accepted for her affirmed gender for years.

Our case was closed after thirty-three anxiety-filled days. We have been reported two additional times since then, and we still worry when strangers show up at the door. I was eventually able to provide some training to DCPP representatives so that they could be better educated when they work with transgender and nonbinary youth and their families. I'd love to tell you this story is a tale from a day gone by and that parents like us don't have to worry about these things anymore. But I can't. We're in the middle of an intense and ongoing political fight where transgender children are one of a few key issues the far right has chosen to champion at all costs. In February 2022, Texas governor Greg Abbott ordered the state's welfare agency to investigate reports of gender-affirming care for abuse based on a nonbinding legal opinion by Attorney General Ken Paxton. Investigations began immediately. Families and children lived in fear while injunctions were filed and the legal system battled it out. Now families are suing the governor for these investigations.

Advocates are fighting; families are fighting. By the time this book goes to print and ends up in your hands, I can't even imagine what unspeakable things may have developed in this area. I know these turbulent times and the safety risks that come with them for transgender and nonbinary children will not be entirely behind us. So make the safe folder. Document your children's development, their gender nonconformity, and their self-portraits. Keep excellent files related to their medical care. Get reference letters from family, friends, teachers, and faith leaders. I hope you never need to use it, but I can assure you if you do, you will be so grateful you have it.

## WHAT DOES THIS MEAN FOR CHURCHES?

It's time to step up—in real and consistent ways. The burden should not be on the most vulnerable to fight for their own care and safety. That's our job. It's what the gospel calls us to do. I know this can feel big and scary, but I assure you it's bigger and scarier for the young people whose lives are at stake.

Find out what's happening in your town and state when it comes to LGBTQ+ protections. Contact your local school district to find out what their policies are related to transgender youth. If those policies are good, thank them. Thank them as a faith leader in the community. People need to hear us advocating for these young people, not in spite of our faith but because of it. What about your state? Do you know who your elected officials are? If not, find out. Then find out how they've voted on recent policies related to LGBTQ+ people. Call them and let them know you're paying attention and that as a person of faith, these are things you care about. Even if your elected officials always vote in favor of equality, hearing from you helps them to keep doing so. They represent you. Your calls and your stories empower them to be your voice.

When heinous bills or policies are debated about transgender children and youth, people show up in mass to testify about how these children are an abomination to their faith. You can show up and say otherwise. Whether the bill or policy passes or not, the transgender children and their families in that room will hear you. They will never forget you. This goes for your local school board, your town council, and your state legislature. Since the COVID-19 pandemic, many governing bodies have ways to participate virtually or submit written comments when you can't be there in person.

Every state has an equality organization doing LGBTQ+ advocacy. Find yours. Reach out and ask how you and your congregation can help. Similarly, look for local community centers or groups doing this work. You can show up with your community at Pride events as a welcoming presence. If you do, be sure to remember you are guests there and be sensitive to the fact that many queer people have trauma related to religion. That is real. Our job isn't to convince them that "not all Christians" are bigoted; it's our job to show up in love, give people their space, and advocate for justice and equality.

Engage your local community. Host educational events or letter-writing campaigns. Show up at rallies. Call your local library and find out what kind of books they have with LGBTQ+ representation, especially transgender and nonbinary representation. Thank them for what they do have and ask how you can help increase those offerings. Host a book drive and donate diverse books to community organizations and families. Raise money for organizations that are actively serving the transgender and nonbinary communities, especially those led by transgender and nonbinary people. Transgender people are disproportionately impacted by homelessness and food insecurity. Tap into social service organizations that work to provide resources in those areas and see how you can ensure that transgender and nonbinary people in need are receiving support.

Advocacy is a part of who we are as Christians. Teach this to your community and mobilize them because I can assure you that those Christians who continue to harm these young people are equipping their people to show up and speak loudly.

# 13 | IF WE DO THIS RIGHT

This has all been a lot—a lot of information, a lot of emotion, and there's a lot of work ahead of us. Depending on what you brought with you to these pages, your head may be spinning. Breathe deep. Make space. Take a step. It's okay to need time to process. Or maybe you've nodded along because these are things you know, both intellectually and in your soul. I'm not an expert. On many things, I've just scratched the surface. On other things, this book will be outdated before it even makes it to print. There's a lot I don't know, but what I do know is that if we do this right, if we love these kids, love them into the truest, most authentic, most known versions of themselves, we change the world. I've seen it happen in my own home.

As parents, Rebekah's dad and I have done the very best we could. We've done some things well, and we've messed up others. We've tried to model what it looks like to grow, to learn, to be quick to apologize when we make mistakes and eager to name that we don't have it all figured out. We constantly seek to learn so we can do better. We continue to listen to the trans community to grow in understanding how best to advocate alongside them. We are always learning what it means to be more intersectional in our advocacy and to dismantle white supremacy. We fail, over and over again, but we keep listening, learning, and striving to do better. And in that journey, we've seen what's possible.

When we loosen our grips on what we had planned for our life and our children's lives, when we find a way to hold what we know to be true lightly, there is so much room for expansion. Children come into our lives, and everything changes. When we get to know them better, when they share their gender journeys with us, things change even more. New beginnings are filled with so much expectation. We start right where we're at, but before we know it, we've jumped from what this means for today to tomorrow, next week, next year, or our whole life. It's easy to forget that a beginning isn't a static moment in time. We are constantly beginning again.

We want our stories to go from point A to point B in a neat little line, but instead we spend our lives in this messy middle, going from here to there and back again, starting over and then jumping forward. It's chaotic and confusing, hope filled and frustrating, beautiful and totally bewildering. That neat little line is what we have planned, but God's work in us and around us is much more complex. Things don't usually turn out the way they begin. We can look at the past few years to show us how much and how quickly things can change, but this isn't a new phenomenon. The world is filled with plot twists and changes of plans, horrible disappointments, and beautiful surprise endings. These plot twists, the surprise turns in our life, these are the moments when God shows up to change all our plans. These are places of learning, growing, and possibility for which we simply can't prepare.

Rebekah being who she is changed everything, for her and for our family. It sent ripples out into our community and the world far beyond anything we could have imagined. Whatever we thought we'd been planning for our life, for our baby's life, God had bigger plans.

On the tenth anniversary of her baptism and two years after Rebekah transitioned, we gathered with our congregation, our family, and Rebekah's godparents. We celebrated and blessed her and her new name. Rebekah's grandfather, the pastor who baptized her as an infant, was there to preach and preside over this name blessing. He has a tradition when babies are baptized; he carries them around the whole sanctuary for everyone to see and greet them, welcoming them into the body of Christ. We shouldn't have been surprised when he hoisted ten-year-old Rebekah into his arms and carried her around the sanctuary for everyone to meet and greet the child of God before them. This is what it can look like for an imperfect church to welcome, love, and celebrate a child for who they are, who God made them to be—whole and holy.

## POSSIBILITIES

This is hard and holy work, but there is infinite joy and goodness possible when we lift up and truly celebrate the gifts of transgender and gender-diverse young people. These youth are some of the most brilliant and wise people I have met in my life, and knowing them has changed me for the better. When we create gender-inclusive families, congregations, and communities, we create space for all people to show up more fully as themselves. Transgender and gender-diverse people show us a clearer picture of who God is and help us connect to God's creation on a deeper level. We don't just do this work of inclusion for the children; we do it because it's part of being the kingdom of God here on earth. Quite frankly, it's time for our churches to look at the world and our youth differently. Our congregations are dwindling. They are struggling. They lack resilience in the face of change. But these kids are leading the way. It's time we try to keep up. Moving from inclusion to celebration changes everything.

When we create gender-affirming, gender-inclusive homes, our kids can be themselves. Little ones use their imagination. They dress up as firefighters and ballerinas; they take turns being the mom, dad, or parent; and they can dream of a world where more is possible than most of us ever believed. Once, during the time when Rebekah was exploring her identity but hadn't found the words to tell us who she was, I was at a doctor's office with her little brother. Elijah was five years old and playing with the big bin of Duplo blocks in the waiting room. Suddenly, he stopped what he was doing and ran over to me with a little Duplo person in his hands. The person had a face on one side that appeared typically feminine with red lips and long eyelashes, and on the other side, there was a face that appeared typically masculine with a base-ball cap. He said, "Look, Mom! This is like [Rebekah]! It can be a boy," and he showed me the masculine face before flipping it around to show me the feminine face, "or a girl." He repeated the motion: "A boy . . . or a girl." He must have done it three more times, grinning the whole time. At five years old, he didn't yet know the word *transgender* or the way his sister would claim her identity, but he saw her for who she was and how she was navigating the world. And it brought him joy! These children and young people love the people in their lives for who they are, not who they expected them to be or wanted them to be. They show up every day as more authentic versions of themselves.

It may seem like gender is all my family talks about, and occasionally it can feel that way. But my kids are just kids. Rebekah is a sixteen-year-old who spends her time managing school, hanging out with friends, and juggling activities. She plays field hockey, sings in three different choirs, and doesn't ever miss a chance to perform on stage. She loves to read and write, and she's already written her first book, *A Kids Book about Being Inclusive*. Being transgender is just one piece of who she is. That's the gift that we give young people when we raise them in gender-inclusive spaces. They can be who they are far beyond any gender box.

Sure, our dinner conversation might include the latest bill that we need to fight or an injustice that happened to a classmate at school, but that's not a bad thing. That's not a limitation. That's just because my children have a vision for what's possible and aren't afraid to work toward it. They advocate for their friends. They point out gender stereotypes when I miss them. They challenge me to be a better person every day.

And oh my goodness, we laugh. When you run toward hard conversations, when you deal in rawness and realness, when you can see both the ugliness and beauty of the world in one glance, there's a depth to your life and your experience of relationships and community that isn't otherwise possible. You must find joy in the everyday because otherwise the challenges would break you. You celebrate every win because you know the losses will come. You hold your people more dearly and more genuinely because you don't have time for shallowness or selfishness.

When we love our kids with abandon, when we dedicate time to getting to know who they really are, and when we protect them from everyone and everything that tells them to be something else, they shine with a brightness that's incomparable. Their authenticity is magnetic. By showing up fully as themselves, they create space for others to do the same.

## NOT AN ALLY

When we do this right, there is so much possibility. That possibility looks like eleven-year-old Rebekah sharing her story as a transgender young person at the 2018 ELCA Youth Gathering in Houston, Texas, on stage in front of thirty-one thousand people, declaring that God does not make mistakes. It looks like the queer teens who ran up to Rebekah after she came off stage with hugs and tears because they saw a place for themselves in the church for the first time. It looks like the transgender youth who came out to their pastors on the trip home. It looks like the pastor who came out as queer to their youth in the hotel that night.

That possibility looks like me. My journey as a parent of a transgender child led me to more fully understanding who I am. My daughter taught me what it meant to truly love someone for who they are and not who you thought they were. She modeled for me what it means to fully show up as yourself in the world. Watching my daughter bravely live her truth and connecting to the wider LGBTQ+ community alongside her gave me the courage to come out as bisexual to myself and then my husband and a few close friends. But I hadn't gone any further.

At that youth gathering, ReconcilingWorks, an organization committed to affirming and celebrating LGBTQ+ folks, had a space in the convention center filled with different Pride flags— nonbinary, transgender, bisexual, pansexual, asexual, gender fluid, and more. Over the course of days, young people excitedly found their flags, took selfies, and shared their identities with each other and the world. It was beautiful and joy filled, and I wanted in on it. The bisexual flag was right there waiting for me. But that would mean coming out.

My daughter and I were at the youth gathering for a few days, and each time we went by all those flags, my breath would catch in my chest. Could I do it? Would I do it? On our last day, we headed back to the space so my daughter could get a picture with her flags. She innocently said, "And you can get a picture with the ally flag!" She knew I was cisgender. She assumed I was straight. I had never said otherwise. I was married to a man, a man I'd been in love with for the past twenty-one years. But that wasn't the whole story; that wasn't all of me. My marriage doesn't put a limit on who I can be. My previous relationships don't either. For a long time, I thought they did. Suddenly, I felt like a fraud. I had become an outspoken parent advocate for transgender and LGBTQ+ youth. I spent my life publicly fighting for this community, her community, celebrating people for being themselves all while I wasn't showing up as my whole self.

I said, "I'm not an ally." She looked confused. "But you're married to Daddy," she replied. I watched the wheels turn in her head as she thought it through. "Oh! But you could still be bi or pan or probably a lot of other things!" Yes. I told her I was bisexual, and a beautiful conversation followed. We talked about identities and assumptions, biphobia and bisexual erasure. I told her that it was her authenticity and confidence that helped me stop feeling like I wasn't queer enough or like I didn't deserve to take up space as my full self. We went back to those flags, and we both proudly took our selfies.

I posted that selfie, of me and the bisexual flag, in July 2018. I came out to my family, my friends, and the whole darn internet.

It's been wonderful and hard, affirming and exhausting. I'm still getting used to saying it aloud. I'm bisexual. I'm openly queer. My heart still beats a smidge faster when the words leave my mouth, but I know visibility matters. People are usually surprised when I say I'm queer. I'm married to a man. I'm a pastor's wife. I don't fit whatever image they have in their head of what queer means, but that's the point. For me, being queer means rejecting the boxes people want to shove me in, not simply choosing a different box. This is who I am. By being open and proud of my identity, I can create space for other people to show up as themselves.

Yes, sexuality and gender are totally different, but showing up as your most authentic self is contagious. Rebekah living her truth created space for me to live mine. The world is a more beautiful place when we all dare to be seen and loved for our true selves. And I'm not alone in this. I've met so many parents of transgender and gender-diverse kids who have come to know more of their selves and share that with the world. I know parents who have come out as transgender or nonbinary. I know parents who talk more openly about their sexuality. It's not a finite process.

In 2021, Jeffrey Marsh, an author and content creator, posted a video on Instagram[1] about people who use pronouns like *he/they* or *she/they*. They described the breathing room the pandemic had given some folks to stop performing their gender for the benefit of those around them and the freedom that came with not being constricted to a box. I felt seen. I was assigned female at birth, and I've always known myself to be a woman. But there's more to me than that.

Still, I assumed everyone must feel good with *they/them* pronouns. They're neutral, after all. A few months later, I was having a conversation with my sister after someone we knew had changed their pronouns. I said something to the effect of "Of course, I wouldn't care if someone used *they/them* pronouns for me, just like you." And she stopped me. She surprised me by saying that *they/them* pronouns wouldn't feel good for her. Huh. This new information settled into me and made me wonder. It felt similar to the moment when I realized not everyone was bisexual.

So I tried out the pronouns *she/they*. I wondered how *they* would feel. I changed my bios on social media to reflect them. I felt a little unsure until the day someone intentionally referred to me as *they*. I was absolutely delighted. I felt warm and fuzzy and seen. Oh yes, that felt good and right. *She/her* pronouns don't bother me. *They* feel just fine. *They/them* feel wonderful. It's all part of a lifelong process of getting to know myself better, and the people around me, including my daughter, have helped me do that.

## HOPE

These are just some of the ways we change the world when we do this right. It's hope. That hope looks like the burning hearts of a group of young people in New Jersey who wanted to talk about how the church walks with LGBTQ+ youth, and so they created Faith, Hope & Love, a daylong workshop with participants ranging in age from seven to seventy-five aimed at creating safer and more welcoming congregations for LGBTQ+ young people. It's now an annual event that grows each year and has been duplicated by Synods across the ELCA. It looks like young people seeing themselves in the church and having the hope and courage to come out to themselves and their families. It looks like the connections made when a family who experienced deep harm at the hands of a faith community finds a new church and weeps in disbelief, knowing their kids can now go to confirmation class like any other kid.

That hope looks like Rebekah, who was sitting in the car with her dad one day when his phone rang. He didn't know the number, but that happens when you're a pastor, so he picked up. The call automatically connected to the car's speakers (thanks, Bluetooth), so Rebekah heard every word as an angry Christian told her dad how he was a horrible pastor condemning his child to hell by supporting this behavior. Rebekah listened as her dad tried to shut down the conversation. When he finally hung up, she said to him, "Dad, you weren't very nice to that lady."

Rebekah is so secure in her identity and God's deep and earnest love for her that she isn't rattled by Christians who try to tell her otherwise. She can show up in love and grace in a way that most of us cannot understand because she's been so consistently, insistently, and persistently loved and affirmed by God and her community. It's scandalous and absurd. When children of God are so connected to their own identity, they can separate what they know to be true about themselves and the world with what they are hearing. Hope is people who can love wildly while still caring for their own hearts, and hope is people who can be challenged to think and act differently without getting defensive or making it about themselves. Hope is what our communities, churches, and country need to move forward.

My hope for the future is not that these kids would be seen as every other kid but that they are loved and celebrated in the brilliance of their uniqueness, the wisdom of their self-awareness, and the joy of being themselves. I want the unequivocal truth of God's deep love and limitless creativity to shine through in them and our communities.

## TAKE A STEP

My grandmother died in 2022 at the age of ninety-two. Ia-Ia, as her grandkids called her, was a fiery one who never slowed down even after a cancer diagnosis. She was known for her love of the stage and a good party. She loved and supported Rebekah from the beginning. They bonded over their passion for dance and theater. I will forever cherish the videos I have of them teaching each other tap choreography in my kitchen.

Ia-Ia was a long-time Lutheran, leading Bible studies and serving her church however she could until it closed in 2018. After that, she began worshipping with a nondenominational church, where she loved the music, the community, and the pastor. This church was not affirming, but she was eighty-eight years old and had found a community that brought her joy after grieving the closing of her long-time Lutheran congregation. It was all pretty innocuous until she shared with my mom that she wanted her funeral, when the time came, to be at that nondenominational church with its pastor.

My mom knew right away that would be a problem. Ia-Ia didn't want to hear it. She believed her church was full of good people who would love her family like she did. She didn't under-stand that this church of hers would not love and affirm her trans-gender great-granddaughter. It hurt my heart to know that her eventual funeral would be complicated by this church with their "All are welcome" message hiding their honest beliefs about who could be married, who could be leaders in the church, and who God called them to be. Ia-Ia didn't understand. She loved her great-granddaughter. What did her church have to do with that?

Breathe deep. Make space. Take a step.

During the COVID-19 pandemic, Ia-Ia continued to stay connected to this new church, listening to sermons and worshipping from home when she could. Somewhere in the increased politicization of the last few years, her church got a little more honest about who they were. Or maybe it was Ia-Ia watching as Rebekah and I did our work in the world. Whatever it was, Ia-Ia better understood the impact Christians like this had on kids like Rebekah, on families like ours. Six months or so before she died, she asked my mom, "Would Chris do my funeral service?" Chris is my spouse. She told my mom that she really liked her church and her pastor, but she had realized they just didn't understand some things. She said, "My family comes first. I don't want anyone to be uncomfortable. I have to think of Rebekah." I finished writing these pages by her bedside in her final days. I told her I'd include this, and she whispered, "Oh, how wonderful." How wonderful indeed.

Breathe deep. Make space. Take a step.

This doesn't happen easily. I'm going to need you to be brave, to be willing to have hard conversations, set boundaries, and sometimes walk away for the sake of these kids. I'm going to need you to handle your own stuff, look at the emotional baggage and trauma you carry with you, and get help to process it in healthy ways so that we can be the adults these children need. And when it gets hard, remember for yourself that family comes first. Think of these glorious children of ours. I promise you, if we put in the work, there is goodness and hope beyond what we can imagine waiting for us. Showing up fully as who God created us to be changes the world, and helping others to do the same is part of our work as the kingdom of God here on earth.

# AFTERWORD BY REBEKAH BRUESEHOFF

I'm not going to lie. It's really weird to have your mom write a book about you. I mean, I know it's not exactly about me. It's about raising kids like me. But as you know, it has a lot of my story in it. Let me start by echoing what she said at the beginning. I've given my consent to every part of it. She shares what she shares with my permission. And I endorse the practices and advice she offers. None of that makes it any less weird to have my mom write a book about raising me, but if this book can make a difference in the lives of other kids and their families, then it's totally worth some teenage awkwardness. I can be who I am and do what I do in large part thanks to my parents, to my mom. She has raised me, and that's saying a lot. Not because I'm transgender but because I'm a teenage girl who can be a handful.

Here's a little bit about me from my own perspective. I'm Rebekah. I'm sixteen years old, and, yeah, I'm transgender. I love field hockey, musical theater, and books. Often when people hear my story, they tell me that I'm brave or inspiring, but I'm just being myself. When I go through my day as a high school sophomore, I don't think of myself as an advocate. I'm just me.

I hope for and work for a day when being who I am in the world isn't perceived as an act of courage.

In a lot of ways, I'm a typical teenager. I fight with my brothers. My room is a mess. And I get super stressed about school. But in other ways, my life is a lot different than your average sixteen-year-old. I'm known for my smile, my laugh, and my look-at-the-bright-side mentality. That's part privilege and part resistance. I live and lead with joy—defiant joy. Transgender joy is an act of resistance. We are more than the trauma the world heaps on us. Whether it's in church or on the field hockey field, in a television spot on Nickelodeon or being interviewed on the *Today* show, at home or with my friends, I show up as myself, helping people understand that transgender young people are joyful, powerful, and changing the world.

Since I went viral when I was ten years old with my protest sign that read "I'm the Scary Transgender Person the Media Warned You About," I've been speaking on a national level, working to make the world a safer place for transgender kids. I have a lot of privilege in the way I was supported from a very young age, and I am very conscious of that. I also have privilege as a white person who people generally see as the girl I know I am. I try to use my privilege and relative safety to make a difference. I speak to legislators, educators, and business professionals about what it means to be transgender in the world today. I advocate for gender-affirming health care. In the past few years, I've done a lot of work around being a transgender athlete. I want people to understand that transgender kids play sports for the same reason all kids play sports—to do something they love, have fun with their friends, and belong to a team. Big topics, I know.

# REPRESENTATION MATTERS

As someone who loves books, I'm especially passionate about representation in literature, media, and curricula. The first time I saw my identity reflected in a book allowed me to feel seen and affirmed in a way I wouldn't have otherwise, and I finally had a tool to help the people around me understand. Recently, I was on a panel with LeVar Burton at the New Jersey Education Association Convention talking about this very thing, and he said, "It is difficult, if not impossible, to grow up with a healthy self-image absent seeing oneself reflected in the culture." That's the power of representation. When we are seen and affirmed by the books we read, we are more equipped to see and affirm other people around us. That's how we're going to create the world we want to live in. I love reading books about people who are different from me so I can learn about their experiences and develop that empathetic connection. Books can bring us together.

In 2018, at eleven years old, I testified before the New Jersey state legislature in support of an LGBTQ-inclusive curriculum bill. The bill would require middle and high schools across New Jersey to include the contributions that LGBTQ+ people and people with disabilities have made to society across all disciplines of study. That means that students wouldn't just learn about LGBTQ+ people in health class or in history class, but they would be able to see LGBTQ+ individuals as full human beings who are present in every part of society. It's about so much more than a history lesson. It's about being seen and valued as a part of the school community. That bill passed and was signed into law by Governor Murphy in 2019. It went into effect for the 2020–2021 school year. That was the first time I realized that contributions I make in society could someday show up in classrooms. I just didn't realize it would happen so soon.

## MARVEL HERO PROJECT

There was a film crew following me that day in 2018 at the State House. Someone had reached out to my mom about sharing my work in a docuseries. They weren't able to give us much information, but they hinted that it was a Disney project. The premise of the show was to tell the stories of kids across the country doing extraordinary things in, for, and with their communities. We knew very little about where the docuseries would eventually appear, but over the next twelve months, a film crew hung out with us for a few days at a time. They came to my birthday party, followed us on hikes, visited our church, and sometimes woke me up with a camera in my room. They became like family members—sledding in our backyard and playing Lego with my little brothers.

On our last day of filming, I was hosting a book drive for LGBTQ+ books to donate to schools, libraries, and community organizations, but they had a big surprise for me. The series wasn't just for Disney. It was Marvel. They surprised me with a video call from Jazz Jennings and a significant donation to the LGBTQ+ organization of my choice, and they welcomed me into the Marvel Universe as an actual superhero with my own comic book, *Mighty Rebekah*. I was collecting book donations to help LGBTQ+ kids see themselves in the books they read, and there I was in a Marvel comic. Best of all, Mighty Rebekah didn't have a fancy or imaginative superpower; instead, her superpower was creating change by being herself. That's something we can all do!

*Marvel Hero Project* was released in November 2019 concurrently with the launch of Disney+, Disney's streaming platform. "The Mighty Rebekah" is episode 5; you can watch for yourself. It's been incredible to watch families, churches, and community organizations across the country get to know my story and use it as a tool to start conversations. But for me, the most special thing has been hearing about schools that are using the episode in their classrooms. I get letters from students across the country who learned about me, a transgender kid, in class. They tell me they're inspired to create their own change, and nothing makes me happier. We don't have to wait until we're all grown up to make a difference. We can do it right now.

Every single kid featured in the *Marvel Hero Project* series shows is amazing. I got to know each of them, and you can, too, in each of their episodes. I learned from them about their experiences, identities, passions, and work. I learned about disability justice, housing insecurity, Black literacy efforts, Indigenous water protectors, and so much more. And for the first time, I had a community of friends who understood a little bit of what it was like to be a youth activist, to have lives that most of our friends don't understand. They knew what it was like to juggle schoolwork, friendships, and making the world a better place. Community makes all the difference.

## THE GENDERCOOL PROJECT

Community was one reason I was so excited to join the GenderCool Project in 2020. GenderCool is a storytelling campaign turned global movement that works to replace misinformed opinions with positive real-life interactions meeting transgender and nonbinary youth who are thriving. Being a GenderCool Champion (that's what GenderCool calls the more than twenty transgender and nonbinary youth whose voices and stories drive their work) means getting to do the work of advocating for transgender and nonbinary youth in community. Through our shared experiences as transgender teens and advocates, we understand each other and relate to each other on a level that most people can't. When I tell you these Champions are some of the most amazing people I have ever met, I mean it. They inspire me daily, and they are some of the most important people in my life.

Those friendships and that community help us do the work we do. In a world where the majority of people still don't know a transgender person, GenderCool gives us a platform to share our voices and our stories—in the media, the workplace, and even at the White House. We work with some of the biggest companies in the world to help them prepare for the next-generation workforce. Gen Z is unlike anything the workplace has ever experienced. With GenderCool, I've been a part of reverse mentorships where we get to mentor corporate leaders. I learned from them, absolutely, but I also helped them learn how to build more inclusive and equitable workplaces where transgender and nonbinary people can thrive. More diverse and more inclusive workplaces create better products, better profits, and a better world.

## WHAT ABOUT THE CHURCH?

I spoke with my mom at the 2018 ELCA Youth Gathering in Houston, Texas. There were more than thirty-one thousand people there—high schoolers and their faith leaders from across the country. It was my first talk on that big of a stage, completely from memory, and I was terrified. I was going to share a vulnerable, personal story with all these teenagers, and I was eleven years old. It was also my first speech in front of people brought together by their faith. This wasn't the audience I was used to, and while my mother and I weren't expecting a negative reaction, the fear was still there. Spoiler alert: It wasn't bad. It was really, really good.

As soon as I walked on that stage, hugged my mother, and found my hot-pink spike tape on the floor, I felt the love. The standing ovations that followed were a bonus. There's nothing like the energy of thirty-one thousand people of faith loving and supporting each person who walked on that stage, including me. Even better than all of that were the stories I heard afterward. People came up to me at the foot of the stage, sent me messages on Instagram, and found me anywhere they could for days after, and they told me how my visibility made them feel less alone, made their friends less alone. I spoke about hope in my personal journey and my hopes for the church and the world. As people of faith, society often tells us that it's impossible to find a place that will both accept and celebrate our LGBTQ+ identity and our faith identity. This experience turned my notion of that upside down. This stadium was filled with people willing to fight hatred across spectrums and create space for the fullness of identities. It was inspiring.

The church should be that kind of community. One of the best parts of a congregation is the diversity of intersections present. While faith may be the thing that brings us together, the other aspects of our identities make our community better. To do this, faith spaces must outwardly and intentionally celebrate LGBTQ+ identities. That bold celebration shows me, a transgender young person, that I am welcome in this community and that it is safe for me to bring my whole identity to the table. I have to come out to the world each and every day. In spaces like school and my community, I am forced to search for signs to see if any specific situation will be safe for me. By vocally displaying your allyship, faith spaces can tell me it's safe to bring all of myself. It also normalizes transgender identities for my cisgender peers. Suddenly, being LGBTQ+ is not seen as a "different" thing, and kids like me don't have to fight so hard for a place to be themselves.

Recently, I attended the 2022 ELCA Youth Leadership Summit in Nebraska with youth nominated from across the country. Honestly, I was hesitant to go. The church is still a terrifying place for transgender people, and the Bible continues to be used as a weapon against us. But I did go. I listened to and learned from dynamic chaplains like Joe Davis, an artist and poet, and Rev. Jenny Sung, a free-range pastor and dancer. I heard faith stories of teens like me, stories filled with doubt and struggle alongside hope and love. I realized I wasn't alone in that.

The summit reaffirmed for me that people in some places in the church are not only willing to share space with LGBTQ+ teenagers but truly believe us being there makes our church better. Even as a part of a family that does this work, even with all the positive faith experiences I have, the church is still scary. I still need to be shown over and over again that it is a place where I can belong. The hard truth is that no matter how much work the church is doing, it's not going to be enough until I can bring my full self to every single faith space I enter. Frankly, that hasn't happened yet. Holding that truth in tension with the affirmation I've experienced, I left this retreat with hope not only for the church but for myself. It's okay to doubt, and faith is not a stagnant thing. Rest and reflection are just as important as active work in the community, and I am not any less worthy when I take it.

## WHAT DOES THIS MEAN FOR YOU?

It is really hard to raise transgender and gender-diverse kids in faith communities. That's not going to change anytime soon. Society tells me that as a transgender person of faith, I cannot exist. And yet when I'm supported fully in my identity in my community and my church, I thrive; I can live my life the way I'm called to live it. I don't want to be held back by how the rest of the world sees me. That's not how anyone wants to live, and you can change that. While it may be hard, it's needed, and it can change the life of a person who sees you doing the work. This work never stops, though. It's an ongoing process that changes and evolves. It's important to educate and ask questions while also giving people space to tell us what they need. It's about making a conscious decision to create change every single day.

Of course, I can also be who I am because of the people who have been fighting since long before I was born, since the Stonewall riots in 1969. Fifty years of trailblazing and progress, of fight and heartbreak, of courage and dreams. Fifty years of folks like Marsha P. Johnson, Sylvia Rivera, James Baldwin, Audre Lord, Harvey Milk, Gilbert Baker, Edie Windsor, and Monica Helms. There are so many more, I know. These people changed the conversation. They changed who I get to be as a young transgender person. I wonder if the leaders of the early movement, those at the Stonewall Inn that night and the days that followed, could have imagined then where we are now. I dream for a day that I can't yet imagine, a future where the work we're doing now—me, my family, and every person who reads this book—creates such a radically different world that it's beyond my current comprehension.

This book is needed. It's really, really needed, and, if I'm being honest, it's been a long time coming. The work of supporting transgender and gender-expansive kids isn't new, and having the hard conversations about what that looks like in faith communities with terrible track records for this community isn't newly necessary either. Transgender people have existed for thousands of years, long before Gen Z came along. I don't want to be treated like an exotic oddity every time I walk into a room. I want to belong in communities like everyone else. And I shouldn't have to defend my identity to anyone, in any space, under any circumstances.

To me, this book symbolizes tangible progress in the fight for transgender inclusion and equality as well as a concrete attempt, initiated by faith communities, to make change. My joy overflows when I think about what this book can spark. I get to do the things I do, live the life I lead, and be the person I am because my parents had the tools—the support, the theology, and the community—to affirm and protect me. I want every kid to have that. I hope that you'll be a part of making it happen.

# ACKNOWLEDGMENTS

To the trailblazers who were fighting for equality and justice before my daughter was born, thank you for creating a world where this book is possible. To transgender and nonbinary faith leaders who boldly live out a faith that is too often weaponized against them, your witness unsettles the foundation of an institution that needs to crumble. To every young person pushing us to do better as parents, as a church, as a society, thank you for believing in us enough to push.

To my children, I'm so lucky to be your mom. Rebekah, my sweet and snarky girl who changed *our* world before you changed *the* world, thank you for reminding me to laugh, for always being up for an adventure, and for trusting me to tell our story. The best is yet to come, kiddo. Elijah, your laugh makes everything better. Thank you for loving so honestly, for making friends with the film crews, and for understanding why our family does what we do. Oliver, you keep us grounded in the now. Thank you for leaving me Post-it Note messages, demanding snuggles, and never letting us take ourselves too seriously.

To Christopher, for fiercely and recklessly believing in me. For being my first reader and in-house theological adviser. For saying yes, to everything, always. For loving (*and feeding*) me and the kids so well. For showing up, alongside me, to fight for a world where families with transgender kids don't have to fight anymore. For never asking *if*, only *how*. You're my favorite.

To my mom, for the laundry, the laughter, and all the ways you help. Thank you for working so hard to keep up with our outside-the-box life. No matter what's next, I know you'll be there for it.

To Rachelle Gardner, my agent, for reminding me to advocate for myself and my vision. To Lisa Kloskin, my editor, for holding my family's story with tenderness, responding to my anxious emails with grace, and being nitpicky about all the right things. And to the entire team at Broadleaf Books, thank you for publishing beautiful books that make a difference in the lives of readers and allowing mine to be one of them.

Thank you to my sensitivity readers for giving your time and your insights to make this book clearer and more true. Rev. Nicole Garcia, you are a gift to the church and the world. Maya May, you bring joy, challenge, and hope to my life.

To Sarah McBride, for graciously writing the foreword, for your authenticity and advocacy, for sharing yourself and your life with the world in a way that grows possibility.

To those who listened and learned during Rebekah's transition and in the years that immediately followed, who created spaces where she could thrive. Thank you to Rebekah's aunts, uncles, godparents, grandparents, and great-grandparents. To our camp families at Cross Roads and Camp Stomping Ground. To Highland Stage and Black Dirt Dance. Special thanks to the Holy Counselor Lutheran Church community, who came along on a journey you didn't expect or choose. For loving Rebekah and our family, for stretching beyond what felt comfortable or safe, and for the work you continue to do to lean into actively welcoming, supporting, and affirming the LGBTQ+ community. Keep going. It matters.

To those who poured encouragement and wisdom into me as my family stepped out in advocacy, those who taught us and led us, who affirmed our efforts and showed us how to do better. Thank you to the late Barbara "Babs" Siperstein for sharing her fiery spirit. To Aaron Potenza, my first mentor in policy and education as well as a friend. To Cathy Renna, always ready with an introduction. To Garden State Equality, for equipping and empowering us in the early days and continuing to fight for LGBTQ+ equality here in New Jersey. To all those fighting for a world where our kids can safely and proudly be themselves.

To parents of transgender and gender-expansive children across the country, thank you for showing up for each other, for being my people, for doing your best to ensure no parent or child has to walk alone. Special thanks to the GenderCool Project and its families. It's a tremendous gift to do this work with you. Thank you for sharing your lives and helping the world know our children in all their beauty and power.

To Jason Reed, Lee Zandstra, and Anthony Briggs, for building something holy for LGBTQ+ youth with me in the New Jersey Synod. To Emmy Kegler, for only laughing a little when, having just met, you graciously asked how you could support me in my work and I blurted out that I wanted to write a book. To Aubrey Thonvold, for being a gracious early reader and treasured colleague. To the golden thread, for helping me become the Jamie-est Jamie. To Jen Lee Reeves, for laughter and wisdom. To Lisa Keating, for solidarity, absurdity, and tattoos. To Annemarie Cook and the very-important-business-meeting crew, for something to do on Friday nights for eternity. To Sister, for being there in the silly and the serious. To Colleen, Kristie, Tammy, Allison, and Kim, for being with me since college and loving me in spite of myself.

Finally, to those who aren't there yet, who got it really wrong, or who still vehemently disagree with my message, thank you for forcing me to find clarity, hold boundaries, and lead with love. I hope someday you find the joy and beauty that's possible in radical authenticity and the fullness of God's creation.

# APPENDIX A

### Further Resources for Supporting Transgender, Nonbinary, and Gender-Diverse Youth

## TERMINOLOGY

GLAAD Glossary of Terms: Transgender
www.glaad.org/reference/trans-terms

Human Rights Campaign (HRC) Glossary of Terms
www.hrc.org/resources/glossary-of-terms

## SUPPORT GROUPS AND RESOURCES FOR PARENTS, FAMILIES, AND YOUTH

Supporting and Caring for Transgender Children from Human Rights Campaign, American Academy of Pediatrics (AAP), and American College of Osteopathic Pediatricians (ACOP)
www.hrc.org/resources/supporting-caring-for-transgender
-children

Imi—resources and guides built for and with LGBTQ+ teens around identity
www.imi.guide

Gender Spectrum—family support resources and support groups
www.genderspectrum.org/audiences/parents-and-family

Real Mama Bears—an online support community and extensive
resources for parents
www.realmamabears.org

PFLAG—support, information, and resources for LGBTQ+
people, their parents and families, and allies
www.pflag.org

Trans Families—virtual parent and youth support groups
www.transfamilies.org

Centerlink—LGBT centers directory
www.lgbtcenters.org/LGBTCenters

"How to Create a Safe Folder" from TransYouth Family Allies
(TYFA)
www.imatyfa.org/safe-folder.html

## EDUCATION

Gender Spectrum—Schools in Transition
This resource is a comprehensive look at how schools can and
should support transitioning young people, including a comprehensive gender support plan template.
www.genderspectrum.org/articles/schools-in-transition

GLSEN—a national LGBTQ+ advocacy organization with local
chapters all over the country, providing student-led, evidence-
based support for K–12 schools
www.glsen.org

Welcoming Schools—book lists, lesson plans, and educational resources
www.welcomingschools.org

ACLU's "Know Your Rights: A Guide for Transgender and Gender Non-conforming Students"
www.aclu.org/other/know-your-rights-guide-trans-and-gender
-nonconforming-students

## MEDICAL

10 Considerations for Finding a Gender-Competent Therapist
www.apa.org/pi/lgbt/resources/gender-diverse-children.pdf

Health Coverage Guide from National Center for Transgender Equality (NCTE)
www.transequality.org/health-coverage-guide

Interactive Map: Comprehensive Care Programs for Gender-Expansive Children and Adolescents
www.hrc.org/resources/interactive-map-clinical-care-programs
-for-gender-nonconforming-childr

World Professional Association for Transgender Health (WPATH) Standards of Care
www.wpath.org/soc8/chapters

## LEGAL

Name Change Project at Transgender Legal Defense and Education Fund (TLDEF)
www.transgenderlegal.org/our-work/name-change-project/

Trans Legal Services Directory from National Center for Transgender Equality (NCTE)
www.transequality.org/issues/resources/trans-legal-services-network-directory

Identity Documents Center at National Center for Transgender Equality (NCTE)
www.transequality.org/documents

## MENTAL HEALTH

The Trevor Project—provides 24-7 crisis support services to LGBTQ young people
Chat at www.trevorproject.org. Call 866-488-7386. Text 678-678.

Trans Lifeline—the first transgender-led and -staffed helpline in the United States
Call 877-565-8860. More information at www.translifeline.org

National Alliance on Mental health—resources, support groups, and helpline
www.nami.org

## CONFERENCES AND CAMPS

Philadelphia Trans Wellness Conference—largest transgender health conference in the world, offers some youth programming
www.transphl.org

Gender Odyssey Conference—international conferenced focused on needs of transgender and gender-diverse children of all ages, their families and supporters, and the professionals who serve them
www.genderodyssey.org

Gender Infinity—largest annual conference in the US South for trans youth and their families
www.genderinfinity.org/conference

Harbor Camps—sleepaway camps for transgender children and families
www.harborcamps.org

Camp Brave Trails—leadership-focused summer camp for LGBTQ youth
www.bravetrails.org

The Naming Project—a Christian summer camp for LGBTQ youth and allies
www.thenamingproject.org

## SPORTS

Athlete Ally—LGBTQI+ athlete advocacy organization
www.athleteally.com

TransAthlete—transgender athlete policies and resources
www.transathlete.com

*Changing the Game*, documentary directed by Michael Barnett, 2019
www.changinggamedoc.com

# ADVOCACY AND VISIBILITY

Free Mom Hugs—empowering the world to celebrate the LGBTQIA+ community through visibility, education, and conversation
www.freemomhugs.org

The GenderCool Project—a youth-led movement replacing misinformed opinions with positive, powerful experiences meeting transgender and nonbinary young people who are thriving
www.gendercool.org

Movement Advancement Project—a map of LGBTQ equality laws by state
www.lgbtmap.org/equality-maps/

American Civil Liberties Union (ACLU)—fights to protect civil rights and freedoms, including those of transgender, gender-nonconforming, and nonbinary people
www.aclu.org

National LGBTQ Task Force—advocacy organization advancing justice and equality for LGBTQ people
www.thetaskforce.org

# APPENDIX B

## *Books as Tools for Education, Conversation, and Representation*

Over the past few years, the availability of children's picture books that include gender-expansive characters and/or messages of authenticity and inclusion has greatly increased. This is far from an exhaustive list but simply a selection of highlights.

Extensive book lists including middle-grade and young-adult books are available from Human Rights Campaign's Welcoming Schools at www.welcomingschools.org/resources/books.

Airlie Anderson, *Neither* (New York: Little, Brown, and Company, 2018)

C. K. Malone, *A Costume for Charly* (Minneapolis: Beaming Books, 2022)

Gia Parr, *A Kids Book about Being Transgender* (Portland, OR: A Kids Book About, 2021)

Hunter Chinn-Raicht, *A Kids Book about Being Non-binary* (Portland, OR: A Kids Book About, 2021)

Jessica Love, *Julián Is a Mermaid* (Somerville, MA: Candlewick Press, 2018)

Jodi Patterson, *Born Ready: The True Story of a Boy Named Penelope* (New York: Crown Books for Young Readers, 2021)

J. R. Ford and Vanessa Ford, *Calvin* (New York: G. P. Putnam's Sons, 2021)

Katherine Locke, *What Are Your Words?: A Book about Pronouns* (New York: Little Brown and Company, 2021)

Kyle Lukoff, *When Aidan Became a Brother* (New York: Lee & Low Books, 2019)

Michael Hall, *Red: A Crayon's Story* (New York: HarperCollins Publishers, 2015)

Rebekah Bruesehoff and Ashton Mota, *A Kids Book about Being Inclusive* (Portland, OR: A Kids Book About, 2021)

Robb Pearlman, *Pink Is for Boys* (Philadelphia: Running Press, 2018)

Taylor Rouanzion, *Rainbow Boy* (Minneapolis: Beaming Books, 2021)

Theresa Thorn, *It Feels Good to Be Yourself* (New York: Henry and Holt Company, 2019)

Trinity Neal, *My Rainbow* (New York: Kokila, 2020)

# GENDER-INCLUSIVE RESOURCES FOR BODIES, PUBERTY, AND SEX

Teaching kids about their bodies, the changes of puberty, growing families, and what it means to eventually be in intimate relationships can be daunting for all parents. It can be even more so when you have a gender-expansive child in your midst who isn't represented in the pages of many books on this topic. The following sources are excellent tools for children and teens of varying ages, for transgender, nonbinary, and gender-expansive children as well as for all children, to better understand bodies in all their diversity.

Amaze provides real information in fun, animated videos about sex, bodies, and relationships (www.amaze.org).

Cory Silverberg, *Sex Is a Funny Word* (New York: Seven Stories Press, 2015)

Cory Silverberg, *What Makes a Baby: A Book for Every Kind of Family and Every Kind of Kid* (New York: Seven Stories Press, 2012)

Cory Silverberg, *You Know, Sex* (New York: Seven Stories Press, 2022)

Melisa Holmes, *You-ology: A puberty Guide for Every Body* (Itasca, IL: American Academy of Pediatrics, 2022)

Rachel E. Simon, *The Every Body Book: The LGBTQ+ Inclusive Guide for Kids about Sex, Gender, Bodies, and Families* (London: Jessica Kingsley Publishers, 2020)

## PARENTING, IDENTITY, AND BOUNDARIES

Diane Ehrensaft, *Raising a Gender-Creative Child* (New York: Experiment, 2016)

Jodi Patterson, *The Bold World: A Memoir of Family and Transformation* (New York: Ballantine Books, 2019)

Lori Duron, *Raising My Rainbow: Adventures in Raising a Fabulous, Gender-Creative Son* (New York: Broadway Books, 2013)

Melissa Urban, *The Book of Boundaries: Set the Limits That Will Set You Free* (New York: Dial Press, 2022)

Mimi Lemay, *What We Will Become: A Mother, A Son, and a Journey of Transformation* (Boston: Houghton Mifflin Harcourt Publishing, 2019)

## TRANSGENDER VOICES

Alok Vaid-Menon, *Beyond the Gender Binary* (New York: Penguin Workshop, 2020)

Brynn Tannehill, *Everything You Ever Wanted to Know about Trans* (Philadelphia: Jessica Kingsley Publishers, 2019)

Jacob Tobia, *Sissy: A Coming-of-Age Gender Story* (New York: G. P. Putnam's Sons, 2019)

Janet Mock, *Surpassing Certainty: What My Twenties Taught Me* (New York: Atria Books, 2017)

Sarah McBride, *Tomorrow Will Be Different: Love, Loss, and the Fight for Trans Equality* (New York: Crown Archetype, 2018)

Schuyler Bailar, *Obie Is Man Enough* (New York: Crown Books for Young Readers, 2021)

Trystan Reese, *How We Do Family: From Adoption to Trans Pregnancy, What We Learned about Love and LGBTQ Parenthood* (New York: The Experiment, 2021)

# APPENDIX C

## Further Learning for the Work of Collective Liberation

Trans Justice Funding Project—a community-led funding initiative supporting grassroots trans justice groups run by and for trans people
www.transjusticefundingproject.org

The SALT Project's "The Anatomy of a Christian: A Zine on Privilege and Solidarity"
www.saltproject.org/the-anatomy-of-a-christian

## BIPOC VOICES

Austin Channing Brown, *I'm Still Here: Black Dignity in a World Made for Whiteness* (New York: Convergent Books, 2018)

Francisco J. Galarte, *Brown Trans Figurations: Rethinking Race, Gender, and Sexuality in Chicanx/Latinx Studies* (Austin: University of Texas Press, 2021)

Heather McGhee, *The Sum of Us: What Racism Costs Everyone and How We Can Prosper Together* (New York: One World, 2021)

Ibram X. Kendi, *How to Be an Antiracist* (New York: One World, 2019)

TransLash Media—telling trans stories to save trans lives, led by founder and creator Imara Jones
www.translash.org

## DISABILITY VOICES

Amy Kenny, *My Body Is Not a Prayer Request: Disability Justice in the Church* (Grand Rapids, MI: Brazos Press, 2022)

Chella Man, *Continuum* (New York: Penguin Workshop, 2021)

Eli Claire, *Exile and Pride: Disability, Queerness, and Liberation* (Cambridge, MA: South End Press, 2009)

Emily Ladau, *Demystifying Disability: What to Know, What to Say, and How to Be an Ally* (Emeryville, CA: Ten Speed Press, 2021)

# APPENDIX D
## Affirming Faith-Based Resources for the Home and Congregation

ReconcilingWorks—information and advocacy related to the full inclusion of LGBTQ+ people in the life of the Lutheran Church
www.reconcilingworks.org

"Building an Inclusive Church" by ReconcilingWorks—trainings and tool kit to help faith communities be more intentionally and effectively inclusive
www.reconcilingworks.org/trainings/bic/

Institute for Welcoming Resources—a collection of tools that support the unconditional welcome of people of all sexual orientations and gender identities and their families in the church home of their choice
www.welcomingresources.org

Transmission Ministry Collective—an online community dedicated to the spiritual care, faith formation, and leadership potential of transgender and gender-expansive Christians
www.transmissionministry.com

The Hymn Society: Songs for the Holy Other—hymns affirming the LGBTQ+ community
www.thehymnsociety.org/resources/songs-for-the-holy-other/

Queer Theology—resources for LGBTQ+ Christians
www.queertheology.com

Austen Hartke, *Transforming: Updated and Expanded Edition with Study Guide: The Bible and the Lives of Transgender Christians* (Louisville, KY: Westminster John Knox, 2022)

Dane Figueroa Edidi and J Mase III, *Black Trans Prayer Book* (Morrisville, NC: Lulu.com, 2020)

Gayle E. Pitman, *A Church for All* (Chicago: Albert Whitman, 2018)

Leigh Finke, *Queerfully and Wonderfully Made: A Guide for Christian LGBTQ+ Teens* (Minneapolis: Beaming Books, 2020)

Ross Murray, *Made Known Loved: Developing LGBTQ-Inclusive Youth Ministry* (Minneapolis: Fortress Press, 2021)

# APPENDIX E

*Liturgy for a Name Blessing*

This is the name-blessing liturgy we used for Rebekah in 2017. It was compiled by Rebekah's dad, Rev. Christopher Bruese-hoff, from a variety of sources. We first became aware of the idea of a name blessing through Rev. Asher O'Callaghan's story. He was then a parishioner at House for all Sinners and Saints, an ELCA congregation in Denver, Colorado. He shared about his experience as a transgender man in the church community, including the naming rite, in a blog, and Rev. Nadia Bolz Weber, who was the pastor there, shared the liturgy that her community used when someone in the congregation took a new name. The liturgy below was adapted from *The Liturgy for the Claiming of a New Name*, curated by Rev. Dr. Cameron Partridge and available on the "Many Voices: A Black Church Movement for Gay and Transgender Justice" blog. The Bible readings included here come from *The Inclusive Bible*, although we originally used the New Revised Standard Version.

## THE GIVING AND BLESSING OF A NAME

*This rite was written for use when the individual receiving the blessing and name is younger than a worshipping community would consider an adult (i.e., they wouldn't be answering questions asked of them in baptism; rather, they would be represented by parents or guardians).*

*Those receiving a name and blessing are presented by a sponsor or another representative to the congregation.*

**P.** The Lord be with you.

**C. And also with you.**

**P.** Let us pray. Holy One of Blessing, in baptism you bring us to new life in Jesus Christ, and you name us Beloved. We give you thanks for the renewal of that life and love in *[Name]*, who now fully claims *[his/her/their/other pronoun]* name. Strengthen and uphold *[Name]* as *[she/he/they/other pronoun]* grow[s] into the power, and authority, and meaning of this name; we pray in the Name above all names, Jesus your Son, whom with you and the Holy Spirit, the triune God, we adore. Amen.[1]

## ISAIAH 45:3-4

[3]I will give you the hidden treasures, and hoards from secret places, so that you may know that I am YHWH,[2] Israel's God, who calls you by name.

[4]For the sake of Leah and Rachel and Jacob, my Servant, and for the sake of Israel, my chosen one, I called you by name, conferring on you an honored title, even though you do not know me.

## GENESIS 32:24-30

[24]And he was completely alone. And there, someone wrestled with Jacob until the first light of dawn. [25]Seeing that Jacob could

not be overpowered, the other struck Jacob at the socket of the hip, and the hip was dislocated as they wrestled. [26]Then Jacob's contender said, "Let me go, for day is breaking." Jacob answered, "I will not let you go until you bless me." [27]"What is your name?" the other asked. "Jacob," he answered. [28]The other said, "Your name will no longer be called 'Jacob' or 'Heel-Grabber,' but 'Israel'—'Overcome of God'—because you have wrestled with both God and mortals and you have prevailed." [29]Then Jacob asked, "Now tell me your name, I beg you." The other said, "Why do you ask me my name?"—and blessed Jacob there. [30]Jacob named the place Peniel—"Face of God"—"because I have seen God face to face, yet my life was spared."

## MATTHEW 16:17-19

[17]Jesus replied, "Blessed are you, Simon ben-Jonah! No mere mortal has revealed this to you, but my Abba God in heaven. [18]I also tell you this: your name now is 'Rock,' and on bedrock like this I will build my community, and the jaws of death will not prevail against it. [19]"Here—I'll give you the keys to the reign of heaven: Whatever you declare bound on earth will be bound in heaven, and whatever you declare loosed on earth will be loosed on heaven."

*The presiding minister addresses the candidate(s).*
**P.** In baptism we promise to live among God's faithful people, to hear the word of God and share in the Lord's supper, to proclaim the good news of God in Christ through word and deed, to serve all people following the example of Jesus, and to strive for justice and peace in all the earth.[3]

"Happy is the person who does this, and happy is the person who holds to it—who observes the Sabbath and does not profane it, and keeps one's hands from evil deeds. Foreigners who would follow YHWH should not say, 'YHWH will surely exclude me from this people.' Nor should the eunuch say, 'And I am a dried-up free.' For thus says YHWH: 'To the eunuchs who keep my Sabbath, who choose that which pleases me and hold fast to my Covenant—to them I will create within my Temple and its walls a memorial, and a name better than that of daughters and sons. I will give them an everlasting name that will not be excised'" (Isa. 56:2–5).

We are here to affirm the name of *[Name]*. This name symbolizes all that *[she/he/they/other pronoun]* is/are and all that *[she/he/they/ other pronoun]* is/are becoming through the grace of God. We honor the name given to *[Name]* by *[his/her/their/other pronoun]* parents and acknowledge that the time has come to declare a new name. This name is the culmination of a journey of discovery and, at the same time, its beginning.

*The minister addresses the parents and/or sponsors.*
**P.** Will you do all in your power to assist *[Name]* to maintain justice, to do what is right, to honor God and hold fast to God's covenant?
**R. We will with the help of God.**

*The minister addresses the assembly.*
**P.** Will you honor *[Name]* in name and in spirit as *[she/he/they/ other pronoun]* continue[s] on God's path?
**C. We will with the help of God.**
**P.** Dynamic and holy God, we remember how you changed the names of Abraham and Sarah as they set out to follow you. We

know that you changed the name of Jacob after a long night of wrestling with you. We now declare publicly and affirm the name you have bestowed upon *[Name]*.

*Sponsors, family, and others may come forward and lay hands upon the candidate's head or upon the shoulders of those around the candidate.*

**P.** *[Name]*, receive the blessings of God, in the name of the Father, and of the ✝ Son, and of the Holy Spirit.

**C. Amen.**

**P.** Walk in the Spirit, this day and always, knowing that God has made an everlasting covenant with you that shall never be cut off.

*Those receiving a name and blessing may stand and face the assembly. A representative of the congregation addresses the assembly.*

**P.** Jesus said, "Rejoice that your names are written in heaven!"[4]

**C. Amen!**

**P.** O God, in renaming your servants Abraham, Sarah, Jacob, Peter, and Paul, you gave them new lives and new tasks, new love and new hope. We now hold before you your child *[Name]*. Bless *[her/him/them/other pronoun]* with a new measure of grace as *[she/he/they/other pronoun]* take[s] this name. Write *[Name]* again in your heart and on your palm. And grant that we all may be worthy to call ourselves Christian, for the sake of your Christ whose name is Love and in whom, with you and the Spirit, we pray.[5]

**C. Amen.**

# NOTES

## INTRODUCTION

1 Diane Ehrensaft, *Gender Born, Gender Made: Raising Healthy Gender-Nonconforming Children* (New York: Experiment, 2011).

## CHAPTER 2

1 "Gender Reveal Party," Wikimedia Foundation, accessed November 4, 2022, https://en.wikipedia.org/wiki/Gender_reveal_party.
2 Karvunidis, Jenna, as told to Molly Langmuir. "I Started the 'Gender Reveal Party' Trend. And I Regret It," *Guardian*, June 29, 2020, https://www.theguardian.com/lifeandstyle/2020/jun/29/jenna-karvunidis-i-started-gender-reveal-party-trend-regret.

## CHAPTER 3

1 Amnesty International, "Europe: First, Do No Harm: Ensuring the Rights of Children with Variations of Sex Characteristics in Denmark and Germany," Index number: EUR 01/6086/2017, 2017, https://www.amnesty.org/en/documents/eur01/6086/2017/en/.
2 Jeanne Maglaty, "When Did Girls Start Wearing Pink?" *Smithsonian Magazine*, April 7, 2011, https://www.smithsonianmag.com/arts-culture/when-did-girls-start-wearing-pink-1370097/.

3 Dennis Baron, "A Brief History of Singular 'They,'" Oxford English Dictionary (blog), September 4, 2018, https://public.oed.com/blog/a-brief-history-of-singular-they/.

## CHAPTER 4

1 "About 5% of Young Adults in the U.S. Say Their Gender Is Different from Their Sex Assigned at Birth," Pew Research Center, June 7, 2022, https://www.pewresearch.org/fact-tank/2022/06/07/about-5-of-young-adults-in-the-u-s-say-their-gender-is-different-from-their-sex-assigned-at-birth/.

2 "LGBT Identification in US Upticks to 7.1," Gallup, February 17, 2022, https://news.gallup.com/poll/389792/lgbt-identification-ticks-up.aspx.

3 Karl Gruber, "Five Wild Lionesses Grow a Mane and Start Acting Like Males," *New Scientist*, September 23, 2016, https://www.newscientist.com/article/2106866-five-wild-lionesses-grow-a-mane-and-start-acting-like-males/.

4 Audrey Sternalski, François Mougeot, and Vincent Bretagnolle. "Adaptive Significance of Permanent Female Mimicry in a Bird of Prey," *Biology Letters* 8, no. 2 (November 9, 2011), https://doi.org/10.1098/rsbl.2011.0914.

5 "Two-Spirit," Indian Health Service, accessed November 3, 2022, https://www.ihs.gov/lgbt/health/twospirit/.

6 Kristofer Rhude, "The Third Gender and Hijras," *Religion and Public Life*, 2018, Harvard Divinity School, https://rpl.hds.harvard.edu/religion-context/case-studies/gender/third-gender-and-hijras.

7 Dan Bilefsky, "Albanian Custom Fades: Woman as Family Man," *New York Times*, June 25, 2008, https://www.nytimes.com/2008/06/25/world/europe/25virgins.html.

8 Selin Gülgöz et al., "Similarity in Transgender and Cisgender Children's Gender Development," *Proceedings of the National Academy of Sciences* 116, no. 49 (November 18, 2019): 24480–24485, https://doi.org/10.1073/pnas.1909367116.

9 Luke 24:32, New Revised Standard Version.

10 Susan Silk and Barry Goodman, "How Not to Say the Wrong Thing," *Los Angeles Times*, April 7, 2013, https://www.latimes.com /opinion/op-ed/la-xpm-2013-apr-07-la-oe-0407-silk-ring-theory -20130407-story.html.

## CHAPTER 5

1 A. P. Haas, P. L. Rodgers, and J. L. Herman, *Suicide Attempts among Transgender and Gender Non-conforming Adults: Findings of the National Transgender Discrimination Survey* (Los Angeles, CA: The Williams Institute and the American Foundation for Suicide Prevention, 2014).

2 Trevor Project, "2022 National Survey on LGBTQ Youth Mental Health," accessed November 4, 2022, https://www.thetrevorproject .org/survey-2022/.

3 Movement Advancement Project, "Equality Maps: Conversion Therapy Laws," accessed November 4, 2022, https://www.lgbtmap .org/equality-maps/conversion_therapy.

4 The HRC Foundation, "The Lies and Dangers of Efforts to Change Sexual Orientation and Gender Identity," accessed November 4, 2022, https://www.hrc.org/resources/the-lies-and -dangers-of-reparative-therapy.

5 S. E. James, C. Brown, and I. Wilson, *2015 U.S. Transgender Survey: Report on the Experiences of Black Respondents* (Washington, DC: National Center for Transgender Equality, Black Trans Advocacy, and National Black Justice Coalition, 2017); S. E. James and B. Salcedo, *2015 U.S. Transgender Survey: Report on the Experiences of Latino/a Respondents* (Washington, DC: National Center for Transgender Equality and TransLatin@ Coalition, 2017).

6 Priya Krisnakumar, "2022 Is Already a Record Year for State Bills Seeking to Curtail LGBTQ Rights, ACLU Data Shows," CNN, July 17, 2022, https://www.cnn.com/2022/07/17/politics/state -legislation-lgbtq-rights/index.html.

7  Caitlyn Ryan et al., "Family Acceptance in Adolescence and the Health of LGBT Young Adults," *Journal of Child and Adolescent Psychiatric Nursing* 23, no. 4 (November 2010): 205–213.

8  Stephen T. Russell et al., "Chosen Name Use Is Linked to Reduced Depressive Symptoms, Suicidal Ideation, and Suicidal Behavior among Transgender Youth," *Journal of Adolescent Health: Official Publication of the Society for Adolescent Medicine* 63, no. 4 (2018): 503–505. https://doi.org/10.1016/j.jadohealth.2018.02.003.

9  Kristina R. Olson et al., "Mental Health of Transgender Children Who Are Supported in Their Identities," *Pediatrics* 137, no. 3 (February 2016): e20153223, https://doi.org/10.1542/peds.2015-3223.

10  Jack Turban, "The Evidence for Trans Youth Gender-Affirming Medical Care," *Psychology Today*, January 24, 2022, https://www.psychologytoday.com/us/blog/political-minds/202201/the-evidence-trans-youth-gender-affirming-medical-care.

11  S. Burshtein et al., "Religiosity as Protection Factor against Suicidal Behaviour," *Acta Psychiatrica Scandavica* 133, no. 6 (June 2016): 481–488, https://doi.org/10.1111/acps.12555.

12  Connie Svob et al., "Association of Parent and Offspring Religiosity with Offspring Suicide Ideation and Attempts," *JAMA Psychiatry* 75, no. 10 (August 2018): 1062–1070, https://doi.org/10.1001/jamapsychiatry.2018.2060.

13  Jeremy J. Gibbs and Jeremy Goldbach, "Religious Conflict, Sexual Identity, and Suicidal Behaviors among LGBT Young Adults," *Archives of Suicide Research: Official Journal of the International Academy for Suicide Research* 19, no. 4 (March 2015): 472–88, https://doi.org/10.1080/13811118.2015.1004476.

14  The Trevor Project, "The Trevor Project Research Brief: Religiosity and Suicidality among LGBTQ Youth," April 14, 2020, https://www.thetrevorproject.org/research-briefs/religiosity-and-suicidality-among-LGBTQ-youth/.

15  Selin Gülgöz et al., "Similarity in Transgender and Cisgender Children's Gender Development," *Proceedings of the National Academy*

*of Sciences* 116, no. 49 (November 18, 2019): 24480–24485, https://doi.org/10.1073/pnas.1909367116.

16 Kristina R. Olson, Aidan C. Key, and Nicholas R. Eaton, "Gender Cognition in Transgender Children," *Psychological Science* 26, no. 4 (March 2015): 467–474, https://doi.org/10.1177/0956797614568156.

17 Jack L. Turban et al., "Factors Leading to 'Detransition' among Transgender and Gender Diverse People in the United States: A Mixed-Methods Analysis," *LGBT Health* 8, no. 4 (May–June 2021): 273–280, https://doi.org/10.1089/lgbt.2020.0437.

18 Kristina R. Olson et al., "Gender Identity 5 Years after Transition," *Pediatrics* 150, no. 2 (August 2022): e2021056082, https://doi.org/10.1542/peds.2021-056082.

19 Jack L. Turban et al., "Sex Assigned at Birth Ratio among Transgender and Gender Diverse Adolescents in the United States," *Pediatrics* 150, no. 3 (August 2022): e2022056567. https://doi.org/10.1542/peds.2022-056567.

20 Julia Temple Newhook et al., "Teach Your Parents and Providers Well: Call for Refocus on the Health of Trans and Gender-Diverse Children," *Canadian Family Physician* 64, no. 5 (May 2018): 332–335.

21 Antony J. Blinken, "X Gender Marker Available on U.S. Passports Starting April 11," US Department of State, March 31, 2022, https://www.state.gov/x-gender-marker-available-on-u-s-passports-starting-april-11/.

22 Abeni Jones, "I'm Transgender. I Won't Be Getting an X on My Passport," *Washington Post*, April 10, 2022, https://www.washingtonpost.com/opinions/2022/04/10/transgender-passport-x-gender-option-risks/.

23 Barbara Simon, "Medical Association Statements Supporting Trans Youth Healthcare and Against Discriminatory Bills," GLAAD (blog), April 19, 2021, https://www.glaad.org/blog/medical-association-statements-supporting-trans-youth-healthcare-and-against-discriminatory.

# CHAPTER 6

1 Michelle M. Johns et al., "Transgender Identity and Experiences of Violence Victimization, Substance Use, Suicide Risk, and Sexual Risk Behaviors among High School Students—19 States and Large Urban School Districts, 2017," *CDC Morbidity and Mortality Weekly Report* 68, no. 3 (January 25, 2019): 67–71, https://doi.org/10.15585/mmwr.mm6803a3.

# CHAPTER 7

1 "Lutheran Introduction to Sexual Orientation, Gender Identity, and Gender Expression," ReconcilingWorks, accessed November 4, 2022, https://www.reconcilingworks.org/resources/sogie/lgbtq/.

2 Gabriel R. Murchison et al., "School Restroom and Locker Room Restrictions and Sexual Assault Risk among Transgender Youth," *Pediatrics* 143, no. 6 (June 2019): e20182902, https://doi.org/10.1542/peds.2018-2902.

3 Lance S. Weinhardt et al., "Transgender and Gender Nonconforming Youths' Public Facilities Use and Psychological Well-Being: A Mixed-Method Study," *Transgender Health* 2, no. 1 (Oct 2017): 140–150, https://doi.org/10.1089/trgh.2017.0020.

4 Amira Hasenbush, Andrew R. Flores, and Jody L. Herman, "Gender Identity Nondiscrimination Laws in Public Accommodations: A Review of Evidence Regarding Safety and Privacy in Public Restrooms, Locker Rooms, and Changing Rooms," *Sexuality Research and Social Policy* 16 (March 2019): 70–83, https://doi.org/10.1007/s13178-018-0335-z.

# CHAPTER 8

1 Emmy Kegler, *All Who Are Weary: Easing the Burden on the Walk with Mental Illness* (Minneapolis: Broadleaf Books 2021), 12.

# CHAPTER 9

1 Austen Hartke, *Transforming: The Bible and the Lives of Transgender Christians* (Louisville, KY: Westminster John Knox Press, 2018), 55.
2 Priests for Biblical Equality, trans., *The Inclusive Bible: The First Egalitarian Translation* (Lanham, MD: Sheed & Ward 2009), vi.
3 Hartke, *Transforming*, 50.
4 Asher O'Callaghan, "In the Beginning, God Created Day and Night," Facebook, October 22, 2018, https://www.facebook.com /asher.ocallaghan/posts/10106508365909443.
5 Hartke, *Transforming*, 94.
6 Shannon T. L. Kearns, *In the Margins: A Transgender Man's Journey with Scripture* (Grand Rapids, MI: Eerdmans Publishing, 2022), 39.

# CHAPTER 10

1 "Who We Are," ReconcilingWorks, accessed November 4, 2022, https://www.reconcilingworks.org/about/.
2 "How to Become RIC," ReconcilingWorks, accessed November 4, 2022, https://www.reconcilingworks.org/ric/becomeric/.

# CHAPTER 11

1 "Land Acknowledgement," Nanticoke Lenni-Lenape Tribal Nation, accessed November 4, 2022, https://nlltribe.com/land -acknowledgement/.
2 Tiq Milan, "First Time I Saw Me: Trans Voices | Netflix + GLAAD," Netflix, June 13, 2018, interview, 2:01 to 2:13, https:// www.youtube.com/watch?v=CPDyN-ygEIM&t=146s.
3 Jeffrey Masters, "Chella Man: This Trans, Deaf Artist Reclaims His Body with Tattoos," *Advocate*, June 29, 2021, https://www .advocate.com/transgender/2021/6/29/chella-man-trans-deaf -artist-reclaims-his-body-tattoos.

4 Raquel Willis, "A Vision of Liberation," Raquel Willis (blog), January 21, 2017, http://www.raquelwillis.com/blog/2017/1/21/a-vision-of-liberation.

5 Janet Mock, *Redefining Realness: My Path to Womanhood, Identity, Love, and So Much More* (New York: Atria Paperback, 2014), 249.

6 Kimberlé Crenshaw, "Demarginalizing the Intersection of Race and Sex: A Black Feminist Critique of Antidiscrimination Doctrine, Feminist Theory and Antiracist Policies," *University of Chicago Legal Forum* 1989, no. 1 (1989): 139–167.

7 Alicia Garza, *The Purpose of Power: How We Come Together When We Fall Apart* (New York: One World, 2020), 188.

8 Garza, *The Purpose of Power*, 187.

9 Madeleine Carlisle, "Anti-Trans Violence and Rhetoric Reached Record Highs across America in 2021," *Time*, December 30, 2021, https://time.com/6131444/2021-anti-trans-violence/.

10 Janet Mock, "Why I Celebrate and Stand By Tourmaline," *Allure*, October 13, 2017, https://www.allure.com/story/janet-mock-why-i-stand-by-reina-gossett-marsha-p-johnson; Tourmaline, "Tourmaline on Transgender Storytelling, David France, and the Netflix Marsha P. Johnson Documentary," *Teen Vogue*, October 11, 2017, https://www.teenvogue.com/story/reina-gossett-marsha-p-johnson-op-ed.

11 Willis, "A Vision of Liberation."

12 Mock, *Redefining Realness*, 256–7.

13 Crenshaw, "Demarginalizing the Intersection," 167.

14 Lizette Trujillo, email message to author, August 16, 2022, based on Trujillo's Facebook post, January 21, 2021, https://www.facebook.com/photo/?fbid=10220991284105960.

# CHAPTER 12

1 Orion Rummler, "Health Care for Transgender Adults becomes New Target in 2023 Legislative Session", 19th News, January 5,

2023, https://19thnews.org/2023/01/trans-health-care-bills-2023 -legislative-session-lgbtq/.

2 "Right of Transgender Student to Use Appropriate Bathroom," ACLU Virginia, accessed November 4, 2002, https://www.acluva .org/en/cases/gavin-grimm-v-gloucester-county-public-school -board.

3 Melissa Gira Grant, "The Groups Pushing Anti-Trans Laws Want to Divide the LGBTQ Movement," *New Republic*, February 17, 2022, https://newrepublic.com/article/165403/groups-pushing -anti-trans-laws-want-divide-lgbtq-movement; Alex Kotch, "Leading Free-Market Policy Network Enabling Anti-LGBTQ Hate," Southern Poverty Law Center, December 7, 2021, https://www .splcenter.org/hatewatch/2021/12/07/leading-free-market-policy -network-enabling-anti-lgbtq-hate.

4 "About 5% of Young Adults."

5 Chase Strangio, "The Courts Won't Free Us—Only We Can," *Them*, June 1, 2022, https://www.them.us/story/chase-strangio -supreme-court-queer-rights.

6 *"Americans' Support for Key LGBTQ Rights Continues to Tick Upward: Findings From the 2021 American Values Atlas,"* PRRI, March 14, 2022, https://www.prri.org/research/americans-support-for-key-lgbtq -rights-continues-to-tick-upward-findings-from-the-2021-american -values-atlas/.

7 Ben Harder, "Best Children's Hospitals 2022–2023 Honor Roll and Overview," *US News and World Report*, June 14, 2022, https:// health.usnews.com/health-news/best-childrens-hospitals/arti cles/best-childrens-hospitals-honor-roll-and-overview.

# CHAPTER 13

1 Jeffrey Marsh, "Trans 101: She/They and He/They," Instagram @thejeffreymarsh, May 28, 2021, https://www.instagram.com/tv /CPbx7rIh-3j/?igshid=NTdlMDg3MTY=.

# APPENDIX E

1 Lightly adapted from *Changes: Prayers and Services Honoring Rites of Passage* (New York: Church Publishing, 2007), 47.

2 *The Inclusive Bible* opts to use "YHWH" instead of "Lord." YHWH, sometimes called the Tetragrammaton, is the four letters of the name for God in the Hebrew Scriptures transliterated from Hebrew. *The Inclusive Bible*, vi.

3 Evangelical Lutheran Church in America and Evangelical Lutheran Church in Canada, *Evangelical Lutheran Worship* (Minneapolis: Augsburg Fortress 2017), 236.

4 The section beginning with "We are here to affirm your name" is adapted from the following: Justin Sabia Tanis, *Trans-Gender: Theology, Ministry, and Communities of Faith* (Eugene, OR: Wipf and Stock, 2018).

5 Lightly adapted from *Changes: Prayers and Services*, 48.